Best Wishes!

[signature]

STICKIN' TO HIS GUNS

STICKIN' TO HIS GUNS

A THROUGH-THE-KEYHOLE LOOK AT MR. PAUL DANIEL STECKLE

GREGORY W. McCLINCHEY

iUniverse, Inc.

New York Lincoln Shanghai

Stickin' to His Guns
A Through-the-Keyhole Look at Mr. Paul Daniel Steckle

Copyright © 2007 by Gregory W. McClinchey

iUniverse books may be ordered through booksellers or by contacting:

iUniverse
2021 Pine Lake Road, Suite 100
Lincoln, NE 68512
www.iuniverse.com
1-800-Authors (1-800-288-4677)

Because of the dynamic nature of the Internet, any Web addresses
or links contained in this book may have changed
since publication and may no longer be valid.

ISBN: 978-0-595-43836-5 (pbk)
ISBN: 978-0-595-68351-2 (cloth)
ISBN: 978-0-595-88161-1 (ebk)

Printed in the United States of America

Photo Credit

To the woman who gave me life and to the
woman who decided to share it with me

Contents

Acknowledgements

This book would not have been possible without the input, help, and co-operation of countless individual members of the Steckle team.

I would like to take a moment to specifically thank the following people for their contributions:

First and most important, I would like to thank Paul and Kathy Steckle. Paul and Kathy, your guidance, compassion and friendship have been invaluable, not only during the writing of this book but for the past 14 years. Your sincerity is inspirational, and your honesty is refreshing. I have learned a great deal from both of you during my time in the organization—lessons and experiences that made the time I spent working on this book truly an enjoyable and nostalgic experience.

Second, thank you to the immediate and extended Steckle family—Brian and Bonnie, Cameron and Kathy, and a host of others. This book is intended as a tribute to your work and dedication over the years as much as it is intended to reflect the true nature of Paul's time in office. In all instances, you were and are an integral part of the team.

Next, to the various members of the office staff (1993–2007)—Bob Swartman, Terry Puerstl, Jerry Lamport, Melissa Snyders, Bronwyn Dunbar, Sarah Trant, Bruce Whitmore, Dianne Henkenhaf, Kelly McCabe, John Kerepcich, Andrew Clarke, Sandy Hamamoto, Adam Michalski, David Inglis, Tyler Frook, Chad Swance; and Kevin Wilbee. Regardless of your specific role or length of time in the office, we were—and are—a team that successfully made a difference in the lives of the people of

Huron-Bruce. You each contributed to this book—and to me, directly—in ways that you may never fully appreciate. I wish each of you a lifetime of good fortune and offer my unwavering hand of friendship in the years ahead.

To past and present friends and colleagues on Parliament Hill—Rose-Marie Ur, Sue Richardson, Brenda Chamberlain, Chera Jelley, Nancy MacDonald, Jamie Bryan, Cheryl Fougere, Greg Kolz, Jason Bett, Kristin Borger, Kevin Machida, and others far too numerous to mention here. Those 14-hour days just seemed to fly by. During those often-stressful sessions, late-night meetings, and moments of uncertainty, something unexpected happened: casual business contacts looked up from their computers and lasting friendships emerged.

To the members of the Huron-Bruce (Federal) Liberal Association's Executive Committee, and most particularly, to Nick Whyte. You have been both a professional and personal asset. Your counsel and guidance have been invaluable, and I thank you for the time that you invested in me.

Next, thank you to my own family and friends. For as long as I can remember, you have worked tirelessly to help me make my dreams a reality. Because of your help and efforts, I have had the chance to live and work on something bigger than I could have initially imagined. I can never truly thank you, but please know that I will never forget your support.

Most importantly, to my girls: I love each of you, and I am blessed to have you in my life.

Foreword

Right Honourable Paul E. P. Martin, PC, Hon. BA, LLB, MP
Prime Minister of Canada
(December 12, 2003–February 5, 2006)

It was just prior to 10:00 AM on Wednesday, November 10, 1993. I was sitting in a chair in room 237-C of the Centre Block, just a few steps down the hall from the House of Commons Chamber. While I had been an Opposition MP since November 1988, I was, on this day, watching as the new crop of Liberal MPs came streaming in for our very first National Caucus Meeting as the newly elected Government of Canada.

I watched as a sea of new faces entered the room. Some were clearly intimidated by the opulence of their new surroundings, while others had an air of dogged determination about them that was difficult to miss. I then saw the newly elected MP for Huron-Bruce, an area in which I had spent a portion of my young adulthood. My wife and I spent a great deal of time along the Lake Huron shoreline, at her family's cottage near Goderich, when we were first dating, so I knew the area well. I also recognized that Huron-Bruce was not a region that typically delivered Liberals to Ottawa. Needless to say, I was pleased to see that the voters there had sent us a caucus member this time around. At the time, there was nothing particularly conspicuous or out of the ordinary about Paul. That is to say that he was neither timid nor boisterous; he simply blended into the crowd. Looking back, I think that I can safely say that November 10,

1993, was the last time that Paul Steckle blended into the crowd. From that moment on, Paul hit the ground running.

In 1993, I was Finance Minister—a finance minister tasked with eliminating the massive $42 billion national deficit. For the first time in generations, a government had been elected nationally based on what they'd promised to eliminate and not on how much they were promising to spend. The new cabinet still was trying to figure out how best to do that, without disproportionately impacting upon key programming, such as healthcare and other vital societal benefits. I had been in this boat before, but I had never been asked to referee so many competing financial requests.

Paul seemed to understand what I was dealing with right away. He was a fiscal conservative with heart. He wanted augmentation to healthcare, but he understood that someone had to pay for it; he wanted job creation, but he believed that we had to bring order to the books before we could hope to spark it; and although he had already set his sights on debt retirement, he saw the importance of dealing with the challenges, one at a time. All in all, while he was clear on what he wanted, he was reasonable, prepared to negotiate, and measured in his demands—traits that made him a good friend of mine.

In the weeks, months, and years following that first National Caucus meeting, Paul and I worked well together. We collaborated effectively and for the betterment of our respective constituents on issues such as the Notional Input Sales Tax Credit, invasive species-control funding, and democratic reform. Paul was one of those people who just never seemed to be off the clock. Sure, he was as friendly and social as the next person, but he was always thinking about how he could best represent the interests of the people of Huron-Bruce. Representation is, in a word, what Paul Steckle was and is all about. At all times, and in all places, he was the MP for Huron-Bruce, and nobody could steer him off the path once he had set a course.

As Prime Minister, I relied no less on Paul's frank and honest counsel than I did when I was Minister of Finance. He always could be counted on for honesty, integrity, and consistency—traits that can sometimes be in short supply in a profession that feeds on the 24-hour news cycle and the power of a 30-second sound bite.

I would not want to leave the impression that Paul and I always agreed on issues. Without question, we differed on a good many things. He was both my ardent supporter and my harsh critic, but he never allowed politics to take away from his sense of humour or his humanity. As a matter of fact, he is one of only a handful of people who ever turned me down when I offered a promotion—something he did because he feared that accepting the promotion would hinder his ability to do the job that he already had. Paul Steckle is a good person, one whom I am proud to call both a colleague and a friend.

His story is most certainly one that is worth telling—a farmer and lifelong Liberal turned representative of the people. His career has been colourful, controversial and anything but dull.

Prologue

Gregory W. McClinchey
Executive Assistant to Paul Steckle
(1993–2007)

It was just after 9:00 AM on October 3, 1993, when I first walked into the campaign headquarters of the Liberal candidate for the federal constituency of Huron-Bruce. I had only recently heard of Paul Steckle, and I knew little of the local partisan organization. I was aware that the local Liberals were pitted against the entrenched, long-time, and reasonably well-respected Progressive Conservative Member of Parliament, Murray Cardiff. I also knew that the Liberals had not managed to elect a candidate in the riding for nearly a century, but I was only 17 years old, and I didn't care that history was telling me that our team would probably lose. I wanted the opportunity to demonstrate to myself and to my peers what I could do, and I desperately hoped that Paul Steckle would open that door.

I met with a man named Cyril K. Gingerich, who was Paul's brother-in-law and the manager of his Goderich campaign office. As he meticulously pored over my embarrassingly sparse résumé, I sat nervously awaiting his polite rejection. I was waiting for him to tell me that I was too young for the job, just as Paul Klopp, the local New Democratic Party MPP, had told me only days prior. I waited patiently and politely, but those words never came. Instead, despite the odds, I was brought on to what was to become an experience of a lifetime.

In the past 14 years, facing a steep and unforgiving learning curve and amidst public cynicism, private successes, and unlimited challenges, I have learned many things. I know that as citizens of this great country, we monitor our federal government's every action through the constantly spinning eyes, ears, and mouths of meticulously polished reporters and national commentators like Mike Duffy, Lloyd Robertson, Susan Delacourt, Peter Mansbridge, and a chorus of other "trusted" media figures. Each and every day, from the comfort of our living rooms and dinner tables, we are bombarded with a never-ending stream of 30-second sound bites that outline the seemingly endless list of scandals, follies, bloopers, pitfalls, and tribulations of our elected and non-elected leaders alike. As a result of this constant deluge, many view our Parliament as a distant and irrelevant body, a soapbox, or perhaps a trough for the wealthy and elite of our numbers. It is, however, often the subject of scorn and anger, as upon closer inspection, a much different picture comes into focus.

From my perspective, our Parliament is much more than a purposeless debating club with a multi-billion-dollar budget. It is a collage of individuals that, with the help of thousands of political staff, procedural experts, and spin doctors, is desperately navigating a complex and frustrating system of national governance. The mechanism is obscured by seemingly archaic and ancient traditions, regionalism, childish turf wars, linguistic complications, international personality conflicts, and a barrage of both complimentary and opposing socio-economic factors. Despite all of this, the system has produced a country that has become much more than our understated national inferiority complex will permit us to admit openly to ourselves.

To fully understand our Parliament, one must examine the components that make up the institution. While I believe that, like Canada, our government is more than simply the sum of its parts, there is little doubt that the individual elected officials are the building blocks on which the remainder of the system is perched. Their stories of frustration, glory, optimism, and duty are the seldom-seen fables that can cast real light on the routine decisions taken by our government. In essence, by understanding what makes our elected officials tick, Canadians might come to better understand the labyrinth of laws that both protect and—at times—seem to hinder us. Furthermore, an epiphany of this nature might help us to appreciate the unique vocational demands faced daily by our elected representatives and, in the process, we perhaps might learn something about ourselves.

In the pages that follow, it is my intention to provide certain insights into the developmental journey that has taken Paul Steckle from his humble beginnings as a Huron County pork farmer to one of the most senior members of the Canadian House of Commons. The basic and underlying theme of my work is simply, "Who is Paul Steckle?"

His supporters see him as a bold political leader whose faith keeps him resolute, focused, and determined; as a dedicated public servant who places his constituents ahead of his career; and as a man whose family is paramount in his life. Defenders view him as one who is committed to his moral duty and oath as an MP over his station or his history with the Liberal Party. His critics view him as a religious fundamentalist whose moral code is mired in a bygone era of secularism; as a man who is homophobic, close-minded, and traditional to a fault; as an ungrateful political opportunist who owes his success to lucky timing and his ability to capitalize on the anger of the masses.

During my tenure with Paul's office, I have come to know that ignorance breeds anger, and anger breeds discontent. We all love to hate those elected to govern, but few of us have ever taken the time or opportunity to actually walk in their shoes or to grapple with the rationale that surrounds their decisions and directs their conduct.

For more than a decade, I have had the pleasure of knowing and working alongside Mr. Paul Daniel Steckle. More importantly, I have had the distinct honour of being a part of the "Steckle team." The team comprises several dedicated, patient, and hard-working people, both in the constituency and in our nation's capital. The experience has allowed me to come to know the truly honourable man who occupies the big chair in Room 484 of the Confederation Building of Canada's Parliament. It is my hope that the pages of this book will provide you with a behind-the-scenes look at both the man and the organization that has sprung up around him.

With luck, this unique perspective will help you to know Paul Steckle as I do and to come to understand how this unconventional man of the people defied the odds and became an uncommonly popular Liberal Member of Parliament in a traditionally and historically Conservative riding. For five elections, spread over more than 13 years, he drew partisan support from across the spectrum and captured the admiration of his constituents and the scorn of his enemies. He constantly battled to reconcile his internal morality with the winds of current political and social change.

All in all, Paul Steckle—first made famous (or infamous) for his opposition stand on the controversial Liberal gun control program—was determined to hold his ground whenever political storms erupted. For better or for worse, he stuck to his guns, and for that I believe he is a truly colourful, sincere, interesting, and honourable man; an ordinary person attempting to do an extraordinary job.

Author's Note

The following narrative chronicles are my recollections of specific, real-life events, reminiscences, and conversations that span the time period between 1993 and 2007. They are intended as a frank and honest account of those events.

Each section is intended to stand alone and to serve as a building block of the larger story.

Please note that all correspondence and cases cited herein are entirely factual, with the exception of names and other specific identifying aspects, which have been omitted or modified in a manner that maintains the anonymity of the individuals involved. The individuals' intent or sentiments, however, have not been amended or distorted. Media articles or other materials in the public domain are sourced as completely as possible (including names) and are entirely unaltered.

Chapter 1

Reap What You Sow

The most powerful ties are the ones to the people who gave us birth ... Other things may change us, but we start and end with family.

—Anthony Brandt

For most of us, our early years help to form us into the people that we become for the balance of our lives. We may not, however, ever fully understand or appreciate our childhood tribulations and life lessons. Paul Steckle is certainly no exception; if anything, he is the embodiment of the notion that we are the products of our environment.

It's safe to say that Paul's family has had the greatest influence on his life. To Paul, blood is not just thicker than water; it is thicker than steel. He would willingly place himself in peril for the benefit of his wife, children, or grandchildren. Family bonds are paramount and forever; his first duty is to his family. The extreme and unwavering nature of this conviction is perhaps one of his most revealing personality traits. It is also the key to understanding Paul at the deepest levels of his individuality.

Paul Daniel Steckle was born into a traditional and conservative-minded Mennonite household on May 10, 1942, in the middle of World War II. His birth, which occurred at his current home in Stanley

Township (near Zurich, Ontario), was uncomplicated but was a source of both pleasure and anxiety for his parents. Paul was the first child of Seleda Steckle (née Shantz) but the second child of Dan Steckle. Dan's first wife, Lydia (née Gingerich), had died just nine days after giving birth to William (Bill) Steckle, on October 16, 1934.

Dan Steckle was born on Valentine's Day 1895, which made him 47 years old when Paul was born. Dan was a devout believer in family, faith, and community. Although Paul seldom speaks of his father today, I've sensed no particular animosity. Most often, Paul laments the fact that Dan never engaged in any of the activities in which Paul's classmates' fathers engaged—playing catch in the yard, going fishing—which probably was because of Dan's age. Still, Dan felt that he had a duty to his family, and this was a value that he instilled in Paul from the very beginning. Discipline was strict, chores were numerous, and church was serious. Roles were clear: Work outside of the home was the man's job, and the rearing of the children was the woman's. While traditional by nature, Dan Steckle was a man who was not afraid to show that he loved his children; he just demonstrated his affections privately, in ways differing from those more commonly used today. Dan Steckle helped Paul to build rabbit and pheasant boxes, he taught Paul how to responsibly use firearms, and each night after dinner Dan made it a point to share quality "snuggle" time with all of his children. Due to obvious generational differences, however, it was very difficult for Paul and his siblings (William "Bill", Esther, Fern, James "Jim", and Mary) to foster a deep bond with their father. Despite his best efforts, Dan Steckle was—at least from a generational perspective—more like a grandfather than father to Paul. Regardless, the nature of the rapport between Paul and his dad helped to shape the kind of father that Paul was to become. He would be determined not to miss those all-important memories with his own children and grandchildren. Quality time together, a hug at every departure, and total honesty have always been the basis of Paul's relationship with his family, and they are most certainly part of the legacy that Dan passed to Paul. Dan Steckle died in June 1968.

Seleda Steckle was born on September 2, 1908, which made her 34 years old when Paul was born and 12 years younger than her husband. As a Mennonite, she was undeniably traditional, but she was much more hands-on with her children than Dan could be with them. She fell easily into her role as the keeper of the house and children. Paul, whose birth date fell on Mother's Day, had an immediate and deep personal bond with his mother, a close relationship that is maintained to this day. She continues to be an important and central part of his life. When Paul was running for federal office in 1993, Seleda Steckle confided that although she had been taught to never outwardly exhibit pride, she was immensely proud of her son. And although she was 85 years old at the time and had never voted in a federal election, she was going to vote for her son. When he won a seat in Parliament, his very proud mother stood by her son on November 25, 1993, as he raised his hand and affirmed his oath of office. In recognition of the bond they share, on May 7, 1998, Paul prepared a statement for the House of Commons that read:

> Canada is a nation that embraces several different cultural lifestyles and groups. However, in spite of this obvious diversity, we also share many common traits. In particular, each and every one of us has a mother. Yesterday, Canadians from across the country observed the 84th annual Mother's Day. Mother's Day, which was originally set aside on May 11, 1914, was intended to be a day for us to remember the numerous and substantial personal sacrifices that our mothers made on our behalf. In many cases our mothers put their own lives on permanent hold to see that we were provided with the developmental tools that we would require to enjoy a prosperous and rewarding existence. If we look back over our history books I am certain that we would see countless Canadians who made a difference to this country and to the world in general. I am also certain that if we were to look a little further, we would find that many of those remarkable achievements were made possible primarily because of the selfless efforts and acts of caring provided to those people in their formative years. Mr. Speaker, I stand here today as a father, a grandfather, a husband, a successful businessman, and as Member of Parliament. I am blessed with success, and I have only one more thing to say—thank you, Mom.

Despite sharing his childhood home with two brothers and three sisters—William "Bill", Esther, Fern, James "Jim", and Mary—Paul always has been somewhat of a recluse. Even in his youth, he resented being forced to socialize and required an ordered and dependable environment. While he now very much enjoys the company of others, he often requires time alone to recharge and move forward. In fact, during a recent recreational couples personality profiling exercise (undertaken by Paul and Kathy), it was confirmed that Paul Steckle is both a leader and a loner. It may seem like a paradox, but Paul has had these traits for his entire life.

As a child, Paul was like every other boy his age. He began school in 1948 and enjoyed an average standing in his class. He liked to play baseball and other sports, but more than anything, Paul loved nature and the solitude of the outdoors—he felt connected to the natural world, and he loved the seclusion offered by the trees and the rivers that surrounded his boyhood home. After a season of tagging along with Gordon Gilbert, an older neighbour, Paul inherited his own trap line; something that fostered his hobby while also putting a few dollars of spending money in his pocket. He loved to hunt, he enjoyed hiking through the bush and he exhibited a link with nature that wasn't shared by his siblings. He even trained a deer to come to him on command. Paul has passed on this lifelong love of nature to his children and his grandchildren.

Another lifelong trait is Paul's tenacity. As a child, he was the one who always presumed to be in charge of his siblings; and, when he thought he could get away with it, he was not afraid to butt heads with his authoritative father. This resolve carried into Paul's adulthood—factoring in to his career and family interactions. On one occasion, Paul's wife Kathy remarked, "Once he gets a thought in his head, he will never stop. Paul always had to be one step ahead of everyone else. If they played ball, he had to be the pitcher. If he played the guitar, he had to play a twelve string rather than a six string. He is determined to the end." As a child he often allowed his heart to lead his head, something that clearly fed his aforementioned strength of mind. As just one example, when Paul was about eight years old, he constructed his own fishing boat. Not to be outdone by anyone and simply because he had decided that the boat must be sturdy and durable, he opted to cement the bottom. When his newly minted craft plunged to the riverbed on its maiden voyage, as one would expect, Paul was unshaken in his belief that his plan could, with a little more effort, be made to work. Over the years, Paul's resolve was tempered by experience, and while his steadfastness continues, today he is far less prone to hopping aboard cement-bottomed boats.

In the late 1940s, a young Paul Steckle caught his first glimpse of a quiet, dark-haired little girl named Kathryn Erb. She was younger than Paul, but that brief glance eventually gave way to a budding young romance. On June 25, 1965, after many years of casual interaction and five years of formal courtship, Paul and Kathy were married. Paul has suggested that his financial limitations probably delayed their wedding day for a few years, but when asked when he knew that he would marry Kathy Erb, Paul said, "I loved her from the beginning."

Paul and Kathy are a strong and resilient team. Together, they are heavily involved in many areas—in their church community; in sponsoring families from war-ravaged Afghanistan; in financially, socially, and spiritually reaching out to Canadian families living in poverty; and in organizing and participating in countless community events. Kathy's hospitality and generosity is an unmistakable complement to Paul's public duties. When Paul is in Ottawa or abroad on business, Kathy often remains home in Zurich. During that time, she visits with and attends to the affairs of Paul's mother, something that is of the utmost importance to Paul's peace of mind when he is away from home. A day rarely passes when he's away that Kathy does not speak to Paul by phone. In fact, the two of them have been known to watch television programs "together," one on each end of the telephone—Paul in Ottawa and Kathy at home in Zurich. Their relationship has withstood the test of time because they work at it every day.

This very first Steckle team expanded on November 25, 1966, with the arrival of Cameron Paul Steckle. Cameron—or "Cam," as he is known to his friends and family—has always been strong-minded. He is a natural leader, always striving for excellence in business and in his personal life. Paul describes his eldest son as "A strong family man, an active member of his community and a constant professional. He is serious and always ready to accept his responsibilities. He has a great work ethic." Paul confided that Cam's childhood propensity for responsibility and obligation was initially cause for concern. Due in no small part to his overall seriousness and propensity for accepting his responsibilities to others ahead of his own wants, Paul and Kathy often worried that their son was missing out on a carefree and happy-go-lucky childhood, but as time passed, and Cam matured into the person that he was to become, they learned through observation that he was indeed well-rounded, well-liked by others, and genuinely happy.

On March 7, 1968, the family again expanded with the arrival of a second son, Brian Craig Steckle. A hard worker and perfectionist like his brother, Brian was, according to his father, "the easier of the two to handle." Brian has a resilient and pronounced spirituality, an undeniable and infectious sense of humour, and a strong set of conventional family values. Brian readily admits that his father "has always been a great example of a dad to me," and he has fond memories of his childhood.

Paul and Kathy's only daughter, Connie Christine Steckle, completed this generation of the Steckle family. Paul and Kathy adopted Connie, born on October 7, 1970, in June 1971. She was, according to Paul, "beautiful, kind, friendly, [and] cuddly." Unfortunately, Connie died on October 10, 1973, as a result of a tragic farm accident. While the entire family was shaken to the core by Connie's death, they turned to their faith. As Paul has said, "You can let tragedy make you bitter, or you can use it to make you better. I choose the latter."

The final component in the current Steckle family is the six grandchildren: Brent, Shawn, Valerie, Dylan, Devon, and Darren. Each is undeniably the apple of Paul's eye. His home and offices are decorated with their photographs, and his conversation often includes tales of their antics. Without question, the six Steckle grandchildren—with personalities ranging from precocious and mischievous to scholarly and fun-loving—are the culmination of a chain of events that began on May 10, 1942; a chain that continues to shape Paul Steckle and impact the decisions that he makes each and every day.

Chapter 2

Judge Not, That Ye Be Not Judged

I want to be visible on the Hill. I want people to know who I am and what I stand for … I want them to know that when the kitchen gets hot, I don't depart. I stick around.

—Paul Steckle, MP
In a statement to the *London Free Press*
December 1993

Question: What do Pierre Trudeau, John Diefenbaker, the death penalty, marriage, the murder of three U.S. bear hunters, and the politics of the former Quebec Premier Maurice Duplessis have in common? Answer: They jointly (albeit unwittingly) conspired to make Paul Steckle a Liberal and caused him to run for public office.

On December 14, 1967, the Right Honourable Lester Bowles Pearson, Canada's Nobel Prize-winning fourteenth prime minister, announced his intention to retire from public life in April of the following year. Accordingly, the Liberal Party of Canada furiously began to mobilize for a leadership contest that would prove to be unlike any other in recent history.

Lester Pearson, while tremendously respected by Canadians in general, had two failed attempts at forming a majority government. The Liberal Party was trailing in the polls to the widely popular Robert Stanfield, who had been selected as the leader of the Progressive Conservative Party just three months earlier. In short, the Liberal Party needed the 1968 convention to be a barn burner; it needed to reinvigorate and reinvent itself if it was to capture the imagination—and the votes—of Canadians from coast to coast to coast.

The race attracted the attention of eight high-profile cabinet ministers. Household names, such as Pierre Trudeau, Paul Hellyer, Paul Martin, Sr., and Robert Winters, each threw their hat into the ring, hoping to become the party leader and—with any luck—the 15th prime minister of Canada.

The April convention, held at Ottawa's Civic Centre, was conducted in the shadow of the American riots that resulted from the assassination of Martin Luther King, Jr. It was also marked by several protests outside of the venue, the largest of which voiced disapproval to the Vietnam War. These events, when mixed with the energetic optimism and frenzied competition of the almost 2400 delegates, prompted *The Globe and Mail* to refer to the event as "the most chaotic, confusing, and emotionally draining convention in Canadian political history."[1]

It was in this muddled political climate that the 25-year-old Paul Steckle first walked up the large stone steps to the main doors of the Centre Block of Canada's Parliament Buildings.

Paul was a convention youth delegate for the riding of Huron and an ardent Paul Hellyer supporter. These factors allowed Paul to travel to Ottawa for the events of the convention, and with that opportunity, Paul took the time to make the trip up Bank Street from the Civic Centre to Parliament Hill. It was there under the shadow of the Peace Tower that he vowed to one day return as a member of the Canadian House of Commons.

From that moment on, Paul Steckle focused his attention on his end goal. At the tender age of 28, after serving on several local community, farm, and church organizations, Paul successfully ran as a municipal councillor in the rural Ontario municipality of Stanley Township, a post he

---

1. Anthony Westell and Geoffrey Stevens, 7 ½ hours of chaos, and an enigma chosen next PM (*The Globe and Mail*, April 8, 1968), A9.

held from 1970 until 1980. The people of the township then elected him to be the reeve from 1980 until 1985, and subsequently he was selected as the warden of the County of Huron in 1985.

It might appear that Paul's political leanings came about as the result of a flashy leadership convention and an ambitious promise to himself, made on the steps under the Peace Tower. In fact, Paul's drive to Parliament actually began much sooner than that.

Over the years many have asked why Paul is a Liberal and not a Conservative. After all, he comes from a traditional Mennonite family, he is a resident in a historically Conservative area, and his leanings and personal philosophies are clearly right of centre. He seems to like guns, is deeply religious, and dislikes the notion of same-sex marriage. When you take these facts at face value, the logical assumption is that Paul would be a Reformer or perhaps a modern-day Conservative.

But if you ask Paul why he is a Liberal, he invariably will open his coat, tap the left side of his chest, and say, "Because I have one of these." To Paul, it all comes down to having a heart. Paul has said that he has spent his entire life pulling for the underdog, and the Liberal Party is the partisan organization that most closely espouses those values. The Liberal Party has the largest range on the political spectrum and, in my opinion, Paul fits quite well on the right edge of that range. Although he also may fit in other political organizations on certain specific issues, overall he is a Liberal.

If there was a single event or policy that first nudged Paul onto the path of Liberalism, it was one involving the importance of marriage and the family. This might seem somewhat ironic, given that same-sex marriage is an issue on which Paul aggressively has fought the party establishment in recent years. It was, however, Paul's pulling for the underdog in a case that involved a potential marriage that irrevocably made him a Liberal.

Paul Steckle was just 11 years old in the summer of 1953. That was the summer when the slain bodies of three American hunters were found in a wooded area in the Gaspé region of Quebec. Subsequently, 43-year-old Wilbert Coffin, an unremarkable prospector in the area, was charged and ultimately convicted of the death of 17-year-old Richard Lindsay, one of the hunters. On February 10, 1956, despite a cloud of public and political controversy that continues to this day, Wilbert Coffin was hanged for the crime of capital murder.

To many, this footnote in history barely registers, but Paul took notice, and it would shape the direction of his future. The Coffin case actually was an important moment in Canadian legal history, as it helped to bring about the abolition of the death penalty in Canada in 1976 (something proposed during the tenure of Prime Minister Trudeau, the Liberal leader selected at the 1968 Liberal Leadership Convention that Paul attended).

At the time of his conviction, Wilbert Coffin was living in a common-law union with a woman named Marion Petrie; the couple also had a young son, James. While this aspect of Coffin's personal life would yield little attention today, in the predominantly Roman Catholic, traditional-minded mid-1950s of the rural Gaspé Peninsula, this fact spoke volumes to the public's perception of Wilbert Coffin's credibility.

Conservative (Union Nationale) Quebec Premier Maurice Duplessis, under immense pressure from American government officials (including the U.S. Secretary of State) and in fear of losing lucrative U.S. tourist dollars, handpicked a team of investigators and prosecutors, with the mandate of rapidly resolving the Coffin case. Given his lack of personal affluence and political involvement, Wilbert Coffin would have been an easy mark for any political establishment determined to quickly put a matter such as this to rest. Wilbert Coffin did not have money to mount an impressive legal defence, and he was not surrounded with political allies that would help to shield him from attack. In essence, if innocent, he was in the wrong place at the wrong time and, in the eyes of many of his friends and neighbours, he was guilty of nothing more than being ordinary. Unfortunately, the rest is, as they say, history. While Paul openly comments that the alleged facts of the cast are improbable, unbelievable and sketchy— that is to say that Paul believes that Coffin was not guilty of the crime attributed to him—his greatest difficulty with the entire matter centres around the Premier's refusal to grant Coffin's last request.

Wilbert Coffin had asked for permission to marry his common-law wife, Marion Petrie, so that their son would not be forced to continue to shoulder the societal stigma and public ridicule associated (at the time) with being born to parents who were never married. Premier Duplessis denied Wilbert Coffin's selfless last request; in fact, the Premier called the request "unthinkable."

Equally hurtful, at least in Paul Steckle's eyes, was that Conservative Prime Minister John Diefenbaker—a career opponent to the death penalty—refused to use his influence to allow Wilbert Coffin to do the honourable thing by his wife and son. Paul later professed that it was "just that kind of heartlessness that made me a Liberal."

And so, on that fateful winter day in February 1956, 13-year-old Paul Steckle formulated his first substantive partisan political viewpoint. Premised on fighting for the underdog, mired in the notion of "the right thing to do," and postulated as a Liberal, Paul began a long journey that would culminate in his election to the Canadian House of Commons on October 25, 1993. His campaign motto, "Priority: the people," was forged in his consciousness some 37 years earlier and promulgated on the steps of the Parliament of Canada at his first Liberal Convention during the country's 101st year.

Interestingly, on February 6, 2007, 51 years after Wilbert Coffin's execution, Paul Steckle was one of the 280 MPs who unanimously called upon the Department of Justice to conduct a judicial review of the Coffin case, under Section 21.1 of the Criminal Code. After the vote was concluded, Coffin's son, James, and Marie Coffin Stewart, Coffin's sister, looked down on the House Chamber and watched as the Opposition parties, Paul among them, offered a standing ovation in an obvious demonstration of support. The surviving members of the Coffin family wept at the prospect of clearing Wilbert's name. Later that night Paul had a private meeting with James Coffin and Marie Stewart. Paul's meeting with Wilbert Coffin's son and sister, as well as earlier casting a vote on a case that had been such a pivotal factor in his professional path and development, was "one of the great highlights" of his life. In that brief encounter, the trio made a connection on a matter that was deeply personal to each of them. For more than half a century, these three people had believed in Wilbert Coffin's innocence. On that snowy Tuesday evening in February, they jointly started down a path towards righting a wrong that had stolen the life of a potentially innocent man and robbed his family of a lifetime of memories.

Today, no less committed to fighting for the "little guy," Paul Steckle continues to tackle issues that, to some, seem to be bizarre lost causes. His active support for the exoneration of Steven Truscott (suspiciously convicted of murder in 1959); his presence in a BC courtroom as a government MP, when serial killer Clifford Olson applied under the "Faint Hope Clause" for early parole (Paul wanted to show his opposition to the very existence of such a provision); and his introduction of anti-abortion legislation (Bill C-338) in the Thirty-ninth Parliament despite the strong reservations expressed by his elected colleagues are each examples of his drive to fight the odds.

Without question, Paul Daniel Steckle is complex. He has a multifaceted history that has shaped his internal coding via certain profound life experiences—such as the Coffin execution. His resulting tenacity has both helped and hindered his political career in Huron-Bruce, but overall, the underdog has clearly benefited from the plight of those such as Wilbert Coffin (as the Coffin case in particular has helped to direct the professional path that Paul Steckle has taken—and helped to hone his desire to fight for the disadvantaged) and the subsequent impact the case had on Paul Steckle.

Chapter 3

Hamlet: Act I, Scene III (Polonius)

I'm throwing myself among the wolves when I entered this field.
—Paul Steckle, Liberal candidate for Huron-Bruce
Shoreline News article by Tim Cumming,
May 1993

Paul Steckle was first elected to Canada's Parliament on October 25, 1993, but that was the second electoral battle that he waged along the road to the Commons Chamber. Before he could run in the 35th general election, Paul was required to win the nod of the local Liberal establishment.

While Paul had been a lifelong Liberal, he was far from an insider. He had detractors, but he never outwardly entertained the thought that they would get the better of him or of his nomination campaign. To this day, I am not sure if his confidence was real or feigned, but I am certain that he was energetically moving forward with a calculated plan that was nearly three decades in the making.

As with any nomination process, camps formed and battle lines were drawn. Paul, who had aggressively and surreptitiously campaigned for the nomination of the Huron-Bruce (Federal) Liberal Association for nearly two years prior to the actual day of the contest, faced off against Mrs. Margaret McInroy, a Walton-area hairdresser, and the Reverend Doctor Rick Magie, a Goderich-area resident and United Church clergyman.

Issues were numerous and, at times, heated. Debate covered topics ranging from agriculture, MP pensions, and jobs to youth skills training, free trade, and the national debt. But the intricacies of the issues of the day gave way to a blatant contest of personalities and blunt charm when over 400 Huron-Bruce Liberals (out of a potential 900) crammed into the Luc-know Branch of the Royal Canadian Legion to select their candidate for what was to eventually be the historic 1993 federal election (the election in which the Progressive Conservative Party—the party of Confederation—was nearly eliminated).

The contest was short-lived, and Paul's obvious efforts over the preceding two years became evident early on. After winning comfortably on the first ballot, he said, "I worked for 29 years for this evening … I went into this intending to win." The crowd, bolstered by his confidence, seemed to sense that for the first time since before the defeat of Andy MacLean some 40 years earlier, Huron-Bruce Liberals might again have reason for celebration. In his acceptance speech, Paul promised little more than "an honest effort by an honest man with honest intentions." Unquestionably, he pushed the right buttons, particularly in a political climate mired by the unending perception of Progressive Conservative corruption, mismanagement and waste.

When Paul Steckle pulled out of the Legion parking lot that Wednesday evening in May 1993, he sped headlong down a path from his humble beginnings to a place in history. Fifty-one-year-old Paul Steckle was now the Liberal candidate for the federal riding of Huron-Bruce.

The next morning Paul unceremoniously launched his campaign for the House of Commons. He reached to his family, his friends, and local Liberals for help. He was about to enter a contest unlike any other. Paul knew that his competition—the incumbent Progressive Conservative MP Murray Cardiff; Tony McQuail of the New Democratic Party; Rick Alexander of the Natural Law Party; Reformer Len Lobb; Christian Heritage candidate Henry Zekveld; and Libertarian Alan Dettweiler—were undertaking the same setup phase of their efforts. He needed an edge.

Slowly, in the weeks that followed, the Steckle team had its genesis. Names such as Doug Williams, Neil Sinclair, Kim McLean, Jack MacGillivray, Margaret Caldwell, David Johnston, Bob Swartman, Vern Inglis, Don Eedy, Muriel Murphy, and Cyril Gingerich began to emerge, hence forming the beginnings of a real (albeit volunteer) campaign team.

Informal media polling in the area had Paul and the incumbent virtually tied, with 20 per cent of the voter support. According to the same polls, the New Democratic Party and the Reform Party had 3 per cent and 2 per cent, respectively, and the undecided accounted for 55 per cent. With this, Paul knew that the contest was his for the taking. In a rare outward showing of brazen confidence, Paul later commented that he should have sought the Liberal nomination earlier. "I could have won the election in 1988 if I had run," he said, confident that a lifetime of preparation had equipped him for an electoral victory that was almost a foregone and inescapable conclusion.

In the nearly six weeks of formal campaigning, each of the political nominees attended countless all-candidates meetings, church socials and other community gatherings in an attempt to sway voters. A campaign is gruelling and arduous, but as I watched Paul, he seemed to gain strength and determination with each hour of missed sleep. He spoke with clarity and passion, with optimism and purpose, and his words seemed to resonate with his audiences. He spoke the language of the people whom he was seeking to represent, and he spoke it with strength of mind. He had a message, and, for better or worse, he was committed to it. These traits, above all else, are the benchmarks of his personality, and they continue to be paramount to this day.

Finally, the morning of Monday, October 25, 1993, was upon us. Paul Steckle confidently toured his campaign offices and thanked the many volunteers who had been so committed to the fight in the preceding weeks. There was nothing left to do but wait. He and his wife, Kathy, had faced numerous elections over the years; while anxious, they waited with their family for the judgment of the people.

Then, just after 8:00 PM eastern standard time, the results began to roll in. Nationally, starting with the east coast, the Progressive Conservatives were facing total annihilation. Almost from the start, the big red machine seemed unstoppable. Conservative cabinet minister after cabinet minister fell in defeat, and the mood at Paul's Goderich campaign office went from nervous caution to frenzied anticipation. As word of probable victory spread, calls poured in from across the riding. Volunteers who had invested so much time and energy were exuberant that their efforts were finally paying off. A Liberal victory in Huron-Bruce had been decades in the making. Even in Québec, where it was expected that the Bloc would do well, Liberals won seat after seat. Next, the Ontario results began to pour in, and then it happened—Huron-Bruce went from blue to red.

It was well after 10:00 PM when a victorious Paul Steckle, flanked by his family, addressed a crowd of supporters in the Stanley Township Complex in Varna. Coincidentally, as the former reeve of Stanley Township, Paul had been responsible for the construction of that particular building; it seemed fitting that he would savour his federal victory in the venue.

The room was packed, and the results had been counted. Paul Steckle took 21,845 of the 49,521 votes cast. Murray Cardiff placed second, with 13,852 votes, and third-placed Len Lobb received just 10,464 votes. The following morning, newspapers carried the headline "HAMMERED," referring to the shellacking that the governing Progressive Conservatives had received at the hands of the Liberal Party and its leader Jean Chrétien. The battle was over, but new and even more difficult challenges were ahead.

As a rookie MP, Paul Steckle began the arduous task of setting up offices, hiring staff, briefing on the issues of the day, attending orientation sessions in Ottawa, and establishing a home away from home in the nation's capital. This all needed to be done by the time Mr. Chrétien, Canada's 19th prime minister, officially took office on November 4, 1993—less than one month following the election.

The learning curve in those early days was rigorous. Suddenly, Paul's personal opinions were news and subject to praise or vicious attacks by neighbours and political adversaries alike. While he and all the other newly minted Liberal MPs were granted a small reprieve period, due to public anger at the Mulroney legacy, the honeymoon was expected to be short, and the new Liberal prime minister-elect and the newly formed National Liberal Caucus were eager to get started.

From the media's perspective, Paul Steckle was now the MP, and no one seemed to care that he was new, inexperienced, and perhaps even a bit intimidated by the magnitude of his new duties.

Any confusion was exacerbated by the fact that the Progressive Conservative Party, the party of Confederation, was reduced from a majority government to just two seats in the House of Commons (Jean Charest in Sherbrooke, Quebec; and Elsie Wayne in Saint John, New Brunswick). The New Democratic Party was reduced to fringe status, the newly minted Reform Party was trying to find out where the bathrooms and cafeterias were located, and the Official Opposition was the separatist Bloc Québecois. In short, the institutional knowledge and historical expertise that is so pivotal to the operations of Canada's parliamentary system of governance was gone. The resulting "blind leading the blind" approach to launching a new government caused difficulties from the Office of the Prime Minister right down to the new members of Parliament.

Paul opted to set up shop in what was formerly his campaign headquarters in Goderich. The office at 30 Victoria Street North was to become his constituency office, a location that he would retain for the balance of his tenure as MP. At that time, the office had phones and a fax machine, but there were no room divisions; individual offices, a reception area, and storage space would be created much later. Additionally, the milk-crate furniture that had served so well in the past now seemed inadequate for meeting with local government officials, constituents, and respectable public administrators and bureaucrats. This was, however, of little consequence, as Paul didn't have any staff, and the local government officials, constituents, and respectable public administrators and bureaucrats didn't know how to find Paul Steckle's office.

From the three-legged desk to the second-hand borrowed typewriter, the staff faced equipment challenges. For a time, Paul had to operate out of his home office, so Kathy, essentially, was his first executive assistant.

It took the balance of 1993 and a substantial portion of 1994 for the staff, and the MP, to find their legs. Unfortunately, there was no manual for opening a constituency office, for becoming an effective MP or for representing the opinions and beliefs of thousands of residents; the only people who knew the secrets on how to do it were the ones who just had lost the election—they had little interest in helping Paul. Their files had been shredded, offices closed, and what little furniture Murray Cardiff, the outgoing MP, had was transferred to Paul.

Eventually, Paul's offices in Ottawa and Goderich were opened. Regular, full-time staff members were in place, and the task of servicing the public began in earnest.

In 1993 Paul agreed to let me continue with my high school cooperative education placement in his office—something that I had started during the campaign. While I was initially contracted to perform basic duties, such as the drafting of correspondence and casework, my duties expanded continuously during my tenure with Paul's organization. Eventually, I assumed the role of Executive Assistant in Paul's Ottawa office, with primary responsibility for policy composition, organizational oversight, partisan affairs, and community outreach. This is a posting that I hold to this day.

In the early days, Bob Swartman (Paul's campaign manager, lifelong local Liberal and trusted personal friend) assumed the position of Constituency Office Manager. Bob had been with Paul during the nomination process and the subsequent campaign. He was a retired businessman from Huron County, an accomplished clothier and an air force serviceman. Essentially, anyone who was a Liberal or lived in Huron County would have encountered Bob at some point. In the office, Bob was responsible for managing the day-to-day operations, for casework involving particularly sensitive matters, for overseeing the local partisan aspects of the job and for acting as an advisor to Paul. In those formative years, Bob was often Paul's senate—a place of "sober second thought." Many years later, Paul admitted that it had not been in his plans to hire Bob for the office, but the duo made an impressive team that was not broken up until September 29, 2006, when Bob formally retired after 13 years of service.

Additionally, Crediton native Jerry Lamport, who had served as sign chair in the 1993 election campaign, was hired full time as a constituency assistant in the Goderich Constituency Office. He had an undergraduate degree in English from the University of Western Ontario, a tenacity that was unmatched, and a propensity for injuring himself at his many weekend sporting contests. Jerry was 30 years younger than Bob and relatively inexperienced in partisan affairs, but he was as capable as any person could be. Jerry continued with the office until 1998, when he accepted a position teaching English in South Korea, but he was unquestionably an intricate member of the early Steckle team. Many of the concepts and ideas that Jerry devised in those formative years continue to be cornerstones in the current Steckle office structure. Paul stated it best in a reference letter for Jerry:

"In my opinion and personal observations, Jerry is an extremely conscientious and reliable individual who has earned my respect and admiration."

Paul's Ottawa office was managed by his Ottawa-born employee, Ms. Terry Staff. Terry transferred to Paul's office from Mr. Bob Speller's office; the then-MP for Haldimand-Norfolk (in Central Ontario), where she had been employed during Mr. Speller's first term as an MP. It was Terry's exclusive job to oversee the operation of the legislative office; to manage Paul's schedule, flights, and overall budget; and to ensure that the massive amounts of information entering and exiting from the Hill office was directed, maintained, and recorded appropriately. It is worth mentioning that this information exchange was done without the use of the Internet or e-mail. Postal service mail, fax machine, and telephone were the only available methods of information relay between the offices, save for Paul directly. Terry remained with the Ottawa office until 2002.

The four of us—Bob, Jerry, Terry and me—constituted the regular staff in those very early months, but the Steckle team has, over the years, been bolstered by many other staff members: John Kerepcich, Melissa Snyders, Sarah Trant, Bronwyn Dunbar, Kelly McCabe, Andrew Clarke, Sandy Hamamoto, Adam Michalski, David Inglis, Tyler Frook, Chad Swance, Dianne Henkenhaf, and Kevin Wilbee.

While the learning experiences presented by the unique nature of the job continued for years, we became quite adept at ferreting out solutions to the difficult questions and complaints that were thrown our way.

Based on the countless conversations that I have had with friends and family members since those early days, I have found that most people are unaware of the inner workings of an MP's office. Sure, there is the obvious—preparing the MP's speeches, vetting legislation, briefing the member for voting in the House of Commons—but there is so much more.

In the more than 13 years that Paul has been the Member of Parliament for Huron-Bruce, his offices have received and responded to literally thousands of letters, e-mails, phone calls, and drop-in visits on a host of issues, ranging from suicide prevention to criminal tax evasion and from emergency passport requests to death threats to employment insurance queries. There even was one attempted murder case. There were occasional callers, and there were regulars. The office staff was subjected to verbal slander and drunken threats of physical abuse, but also received sincere gifts of thanks at Christmas. All in all, the office staff never knew exactly what would show up on the radar screen each day. Perhaps that is what made it interesting during that very first year.

Chapter 4

A Tiger by the Tail

Corporal punishment must be introduced for those who choose
not to be governed by more conventional methods. A return to
law and order must again be realized.

—Paul Steckle, MP, Huron-Bruce
In a statement in the House of Commons
Wednesday, May 11, 1994

In early 1994, the small, quiet, rural town of Clifford, Ontario, was jolted
by the brutal murder of area resident Joan Heimbeker. The shock and
reverberations of this heinous crime rocked residents from across the
region, even as it renewed and emboldened a national outcry for stiffer
penalties for those who violate the security of our homes and persons.

Huron-Bruce, while exclusively rural and by extension generally
immune from such terrible crimes, led the charge by demanding an immediate criminal code sentencing review, a call that landed quickly and
squarely on the desk of the newly elected MP. In a constituency where a
handshake is seen as a legally binding contract, and houses and cars are left
unlocked at all times, people recoiled at the thought that they might not
be safe in their own homes or on the streets of their towns or rural conces-
sions. They demanded rapid action from their government.

Paul Steckle is a conventional, old-school, right-of-centre politician. He is a product of his environment; his views and philosophies tend to correspond with those of his Huron County-born neighbours. While his personality is undeniably one of a "dove" rather than a "hawk," when it comes to matters involving his family or families in general, Paul's peaceful, laid-back attitude becomes one of a mother bear protecting her cubs.

In response to the growing public perception that serious crime was on the rise—and to the need for stiffer penalties—and fuelled by sensationalized media stories of American Michael Fay—a youth sentenced to the lash for running afoul of the justice system in Singapore, Paul Steckle stood before national television cameras and made a brief, sincere but highly controversial statement in the House of Commons on Monday, April 18, 1994:

Mr. Speaker, recently a small, close-knit community in my riding was shocked at the brutal killing of one of its own, Miss Joan Heimbeker of Clifford, Ontario. Her parents have lost a daughter, the community has lost a friend, and society has lost the potential of a shining young star. The recent string of violent crime across the country has disturbed the friendly and safe country which we all love. We, as Canadian law makers, must take concrete action to ensure that there is proper punishment and deterrents to crimes like this. We must recognize the sorrow and anguish felt by the victims' families, and give them quick but fair justice so that they may try to resume their lives without their loved ones. Canadians look to their government to provide the judicial system with the appropriate laws to deal with the realities of today. Society needs to know that it is being protected from violent offenders and that those violent offenders are given stiff sentences for the crimes they commit. The return of corporal punishment must be revisited as a deterrent to these acts of atrocity.

With those 60 seconds of verbiage, Paul touched off a local and national debate that was to linger for the balance of his first term in office.

Almost immediately the national media labelled Paul as the red-neck, backwoods member of Parliament for the riding of yokel. Suggestions that he was a proponent of abuse and child beating were levelled straight away. No one bothered to ask Paul if he genuinely was suggesting the idea of corporal punishment. In fact, he simply was advocating for judicial reform by pointing out that the current system was ineffective and so vastly out of touch that citizens were prepared to entertain almost anything, no matter how drastic. The national media offered their own indictment of Paul as a brutal radical; someone who was socially isolated and incapable of grasping the complexities of the criminal justice and penal systems.

Nothing could have been further from the truth. When asked why he decided to speak out on the issue of corporal punishment, Paul said that for as long as he could remember, people had spoken informally on the subject of criminal justice reform, but "no one had the guts to say anything publicly ... I couldn't have sat in the House for four or five years without speaking out on the issue."[1]

He went on to say that there are people in our society who refuse to be governed by the rules of good conduct. "Criminals repeatedly violate the security that we hold dear, and our current justice and penal systems are left wanting. True order cannot be achieved if we fail to act to protect those who cannot protect themselves ... For those who repeatedly and violently breach our laws, we must up the ante, and to do this, I propose corporal punishment ... If someone has a better way of dealing with [repeat crime], one that works on limited dollars, I want to hear about it."[2]

The response in Huron-Bruce, both in the media and on the street, was substantially different than it was in Ottawa. There were those who were opposed to the concept of corporal punishment, to be sure, but there also was a substantial number of people who thought that the idea was worthy of consideration and even implementation.

Petitions, signed by hundreds of supportive residents, materialized across the riding; media pundits found themselves overwhelmed with fodder, and constituents grasped the concept as a desperate, last-ditch cure for what ailed society in general.

1. Paul Steckle, MP, in conversation with Catherine O'Brien, (staff of *The Exeter Times Advocate*), May 1994.
2. Paul Steckle, MP, in a press statement released to Huron-Bruce media sources, May 11, 1994.

In the midst of the debate, Shirley J. Keller, writing for *Focus* magazine, asked her readers, "Would Singapore's solutions [referencing the fact that Singapore employs corporal punishment as a penalty for certain crimes such as vandalism] for vandalism make Canada a better place to live?" In response, an astounding 94 per cent unreservedly said yes. With comments such as "There is a surplus of bleeding hearts and a complete absence of bleeding bums" and "Today's young offenders are laughing at our justice system and literally getting away with murder," the survey seemed to capture the very essence of what Huron-Bruce voters were privately thinking. Even of the 6 per cent who opposed the notion, it was recorded that only one person rejected the idea outright; the others simply articulated their concerns with caning in its harshest form; not with the concept of institutionalizing some variant form of corporal punishment in general.[3]

The media interest went on in a seemingly never-ending stream of letters to the editor. William D. Pero of Goderich wrote, "You ask if Singapore-style caning would help in Canada. In my personal opinion, yes, it would." In yet another letter to the editor, Debra Scherle of Clinton wrote, "Whatever we're doing is not working. We definitely have to look at alternatives before we will see a decline in criminal behaviour."[4]

Even corporal punishment opponent Patrick Raftis, in his column "From This Angle," stated, "There's no question that Canada's justice system is in need of some reform—to put some teeth into the system and inspire a renewed respect for law and order."[5]

In short, regardless of whether or not people agreed with the concept of caning, as administered to Michael Fay in Singapore, there was nearly universal acceptance of the notion that the justice and penal systems were not

---

3. Information compiled and cited by Shirley J. Keller (*The Focus Magazine*), May 1994.
4. Letters published in *The Focus Magazine* (article—Dare to Discipline), May 1994.
5. Patrick Raftis (*The Lakeshore Advance*—From This Angle by Patrick Raftis; Corporal punishment no answer), May 1994.

functioning properly and that alternatives must be examined and put into action without delay.

For his part, Paul Steckle led the charge. "The present system doesn't work anymore," he said. "People are coming back on the second and third offences, and all we are doing is tapping their wrists."

Paul Steckle was perceptive enough to recognize that the winds of change were blowing, and he responded to the wishes of his electors in a way that few other seasoned MPs (let alone a first-term government back-bencher) would have had the grit to do. "I'm prepared to see this through to law, but it can't happen if people don't speak out in numbers," he said.

Paul stuck out his neck, knowing full well that the guillotine might fall. Those closest to him privately suggested that he might have bitten off more than he could chew. To many, the idea that caning could or would be utilized as either a deterrent or as a corrective tool in the Canadian justice system was absurd and nearly inconceivable, but to Paul, the very existence of the debate illustrated that the current system was broken and that the citizenry wanted change. Faced with this reality and touched by the recent Heimbeker tragedy, sitting on his hands was simply not an option.

The corporal punishment debate soon faded from public consciousness, but the overall desire for change did not. In response to this renewed public demand for safer homes and streets, during his elected career Paul has continuously adopted positions that veered from conventional thinking on criminal justice matters. He has made no secret of his belief that protecting people in their homes, schools, churches and places of business should be a top priority for any elected official or government by saying "If we can't protect those who can't protect themselves, just what kind of people are we?"

It might be said that the events surrounding the corporal punishment debate of 1994 were the first in what was to be a series of character trials for Paul Steckle as the MP for Huron-Bruce.

Chapter 5

A. Rock and a Hard Place

I'm happy. It's over.

—Prime Minister Jean Chrétien
Referring to the political battle over Bill C-68
Tuesday, June 14, 1995

On Tuesday, February 14, 1995, the National Liberal Rural Caucus gathered for a morning strategy meeting; the House of Commons Standing Committee on Agriculture and Agri-Food met to hear witnesses on various issues of the day; and Paul Steckle began polishing a speech that he was slated to deliver on the Commons floor later that day. By all outward indications, the day was unfolding just like countless before it in the nation's capital.

Despite the apparent calm and normality, Valentine's Day 1995 was to be anything but typical or tranquil. Quite to the contrary, that February 14 became a critical and defining moment for Paul Steckle and his fledgling federal political career; it was a day that would set into motion a chain of events that would have repercussions for years to come.

This story actually began several years earlier, on December 6, 1989, shortly after 5:00 PM, when a deeply disturbed Marc Lépine entered Montreal's École Polytechnique and began shooting innocent young women at random. École Polytechnique is an engineering school that had rejected Lépine's entrance application. Despite the fact that he had not completed certain prerequisite coursework, he blamed his failure to qualify for admittance on affirmative action. With that single misguided thought rooted deeply in his profoundly deranged psyche, he set into action a terrible plan to exact his revenge on society, the school, and women in general.

Lépine initially entered a mechanical engineering class at the school. He forced the men out of the room at gunpoint and subsequently began screaming that feminists were the enemy. With that chilling war cry, he savagely opened fire.

He moved from room to room, shooting indiscriminately and roaring fanatically. Before the day was over, Lépine had killed 14 women, wounded 13 others, and ultimately committed suicide.

To suggest that the scene was horrific would be an egregious understatement. People from across Canada and all of North America were profoundly shocked by such carnage. It cast a shadow over our sense of confidence at its most basic level, as the safety and security of our schools was now uncertain. The resulting questions spiralled in every direction.

The aftermath saw the tearful funerals of Geneviève Bergeron, Hélène Colgan, Nathalie Croteau, Barbara Daigneault, Anne-Marie Edward, Maud Haviernick, Maryse Laganière, Maryse Leclair, Anne-Marie Lemay, Sonia Pelletier, Michèle Richard, Annie St-Arneault, Annie Turcotte, and Barbara Klucznik-Widajewicz; the onset of post-traumatic stress disorder among some survivors; and the genesis of a new, powerful, and effectual gun control lobby.

That effort, humbly commencing in the wake of the École Polytechnique tragedy, brought profound changes to Canada's gun laws. Suddenly, in the eyes of most urban dwellers, guns and gun owners took on an ominous façade, one that (according to some) needed to be eliminated in order to regain the societal innocence that had been stolen at gunpoint. The battle took on an emotional charge that inevitably found its way on to the national political stage, culminating in a Liberal Red Book promise in the federal election campaign of 1993.

The federal Liberals, eager to win seats in Quebec and savvy enough to understand the obvious political opportunity that was presented, promised to "strengthen our gun control laws." The Red Book, under the section titled "Safe Homes, Safe Streets," promised that "a Liberal government will strengthen our gun control laws." Those nine words seemed unambiguous and even minor in the much-touted 112-page document. After all, conventional wisdom would seem to indicate, particularly in the wake of the École Polytechnique shooting, that most reasonable people would want to promote improvements designed to strengthen Canada's regulatory structures governing the private ownership of firearms. While the specifics of the plan were absent from the Red Book, the broad rationale behind the 1993 promise was simple; who in Canada doesn't support gun control?

In the preceding half-century, successive Canadian governments drafted and implemented a series of increasingly stringent domestic gun-control laws. Everything from safe storage and trigger locks to hunter training and range regulations had been instituted, as the political climate dictated. In nearly every instance, the new measures were accepted by Canadian gun owners and by society in general. In the election of 1993, the Liberal candidate for Huron-Bruce was aware of the platform commitments on gun control. He supported the general concept of effective firearms control, but he could never have fathomed the scope of what Mr. Chrétien had planned.

After winning the 1993 election, Prime Minister Chrétien, along with his colleague and Minister of Justice Alan Rock, conceived and put into operation one of the most comprehensive and far-reaching gun control packages in Canadian history. That package, known to the Thirty-fifth Parliament as Bill C-68, contained a range of new provisions, including:

- mandatory minimum penalties for those convicted of certain designated firearms offences;

- a continuously monitored owner-licensing system that included full mental and criminal background checks;

- stipulations that permitted police to conduct searches of private property without a warrant; and

- the institution of the national registry of firearms.

Bill C-68 was presented to the members of the Thirty-fifth Parliament of Canada on Valentine's Day 1995. While it was not wrapped with a ribbon, Paul Steckle believed that it would be the kiss of death for legal gun owners. Almost immediately following the introduction to the House of Commons of Bill C-68, Paul's offices in Goderich and Ottawa were flooded with angry calls, letters, and faxes. Phrases like "registration will lead to confiscation" suddenly made it into the vernacular of local hunters and sportsmen alike. In the riding of Huron-Bruce, people were genuinely concerned with the prospect that under Bill C-68, the police would have the power to enter and search private homes without a lawful warrant or court order. More specifically, the calls, faxes and letter received at Paul's offices overwhelmingly indicated that people were afraid that once they registered their guns, the government would move to ban certain firearms and then would confiscate privately owned models using the registry as a road map to ferret out the specific guns. Most of all, people did not accept that putting a number on a gun would make it safer than a gun without a number, and they believed that the money that was to be spent on the registry would be better utilized to bolster police forces across Canada.

Justice Minister Alan Rock, who was enthusiastically and unconditionally backed by the prime minister, moved ahead, despite the opposition forming within the Liberal caucus, most particularly in the National Liberal Rural Caucus. In the years that followed, Bill C-68 became a key symbol of the rural/urban divide in Canada.

In the constituency of Huron-Bruce, these concerns did not go unnoticed. Paul Steckle, an MP with fewer than 14 months of on-the-job experience, was beginning to feel his neck in the face of overwhelmingly vigorous resistance to his party's legislative package. Failure to act decisively on this issue would almost certainly put an end to Paul's federal political career. On the other side of the coin, voting against the government would have career consequences too. Regardless of the fact that Paul was a hunter himself, he had promised that his priority would be the people of Huron-Bruce, and his personal code was not going to let him forget that pledge now.

When Paul Steckle stood in the House of Commons to address Bill C-68, it didn't take long for those responsible for crafting the bill, the prime minister and the Minister of Justice, to spin angrily in their seats to face the defiant rookie Liberal MP. In his speech, Paul made several points:

> As I have mentioned before, these proposals prompted a massive outcry in my constituency and, in response to that, I have spoken and met with many groups and individuals in an attempt to acquire an understanding of their views ... As an avid hunter and sportsman, I am pleased to recognize the government for taking the initiative to punish individuals for illegal use of firearms. However, I am not able to support further restrictions being placed on the legitimate and safe gun owner....
>
> The process of putting the legal aspects of this bill into place has only now just begun, and unless the new law is successfully implemented, the changes contained in this legislation run the risk of becoming little more than symbolic gestures by the government, to satisfy public opinion. Good policy development and the delivery of adequate laws also include effective implementation and enforcement. There has not been enough time for the regulations contained in C-17 [the last gun control package to be passed by the House] to be fully realized, and thus the effectiveness of the regulations is also not fully understood. One can therefore reason that if this is true that it is also too early to impose or evaluate the effectiveness of further controls, such as a national registration system, which would require yet more time and would place further stress on the already sparse financial resources of the nation's taxpayers.
>
> There are clearly constraints in public funding when it comes to our police forces—forces who are already responsible for protecting our citizens under other provisions of the criminal code. It has been estimated by the Justice Department that implementation of a registration system could cost up to 85 million dollars, with an annual maintenance cost of 10 million, not considering annual increases. Public safety will only be endangered if we dilute our resources. Because of this we, as members of Parliament, must take care in allocating the limited funds that we have in this area to ensure that they are spent in the most effective and

practical way possible ... Secondly, Mr. Speaker, as a legitimate gun owner myself, I am already subjected to a large number of controls.

By law, to purchase a firearm I must complete a Firearm Acquisition Certificate course and pass a formal examination. I must submit to a thorough police examination of my social, employment, and psychological history, and I must also provide the police with character references that they can investigate to ensure that I will use my firearms in a responsible manner. In addition, there is a mandatory 28-day waiting period before I receive my FAC with picture identification. If I wish to hunt, I must first pass a mandatory hunting course, which covers firearm handling and safety. I must then also submit to a provincially regulated test, which further reiterates these points. In addition to these regulations the province of Ontario has strict ammunition purchasing regulations in effect. Once I have the gun and the legal ability to hunt, I must then adhere to stringent laws regarding separate storage of the firearm and the ammunition under lock and key, rigid transportation standards and tough guidelines for using firearms. This clearly demonstrates how heavily the legitimate gun owner is already regulated. These regulations, like all gun control regulations, are very difficult to enforce.

The police simply can not search each household to see if these rules are being observed. The UN estimates that firearm owners represent approximately 27 per cent of the Canadian population, or 7 million people, owning up to 27 million firearms. Perhaps the government should concentrate its efforts on implementing innovative and cost-effective methods of enforcing the laws currently in place ... Mr. Speaker, I would argue that crime control would be a more effective method of attaining further public security.

We must punish the criminal element and leave the law-abiding citizens alone. Firearms owners possess and use their firearms in a safe and responsible manner and do not contribute to crime or violent death and injury statistics. In addition, the Canadian Centre for Justice Statistics reports that in 1991, two-thirds of all accused murderers were known to have criminal records, the majority for previous violent offences, and were already prohibited from legally owning or acquiring a firearm. To further illustrate my point of the small number of firearms involved in deaths in this country, I would offer the fact that in 1991, only one person out of every four hundred thousand Canadians died as a result of a fatal gun accident, compared to one person out of every fourteen thousand who died as a result of a fall.

I am suggesting that we have adequate controls in place, but we are simply not enforcing them … Studies also indicate that at least one-half of all accidental shootings involved the consumption of alcohol just prior to the incident.

How, Mr. Speaker, will a registration system prevent this from occurring? Canadians must bear the responsibility of using their firearms in a responsible manner; the Government of Canada cannot shoulder the entire burden. We, Mr. Speaker, must congratulate firearms owners in this nation for their initiatives into the area of the safe handling of firearms, not condemn them for their efforts.

In Canada, while firearm ownership has increased, the accidental death rate has been reduced by 80 per cent between 1966 and 1991.

In conclusion, Mr. Speaker, people are demanding that we take action to further protect them from violent crime and other illegal activities present in certain areas of our society. The problem that the Minister and, indeed, the entire government faces is the question of what response is most appropriate. In his recent report, the Auditor General expressed concerns over the lack of evidence to justify the fact that the Canadian government has passed more gun control legislation between 1977 and 1995 than it has in the entire preceding 50 years. The Auditor General also questioned the enforceability of the laws contained in Bill C-17. He also expressed anxiety over the lack of uniformity across the country regarding the FAC screening system.

These concerns are only a few expressed by the Auditor General and others concerned with this issue. I would call upon the Minister to consider the Auditor General's comments and the comments of all Canadians.

Hunters and collectors compose a large part of our population and generate revenue for our economy each year through licensing fees, conservation efforts, and the recreational hunting industry. Canada's first European explorers were *courier de bois*, who served the vital function of opening the new world to settlers. Hunting and responsible gun ownership is an intricate part of our rich heritage. I suggest to the Minister and to the House that firearms can co-exist with all Canadians in an allegorical "guns *and* roses" relationship, respecting individual rights and privileges without further imposing unnecessary, cumbersome, and expensive regulations on legitimate firearms owners and our nation's finances.[1]

---

1. Paul Steckle, MP, in a speech presented in the House of Commons, 1995.

With that one statement, Paul Steckle was again drawn into a political hullabaloo that was to surround and, in part, define him for the duration of his career in Ottawa.

Initially, there was a definite cold-shoulder treatment from the front benches of the party. Paul Steckle was again tagged by the media as a redneck for daring to suggest that the motivation behind the registry might not be as pure as Canadians had been led to believe. Officials at the Justice Department scoffed at the notion that this silly farmer might know what he was talking about; after all, they were highly accomplished lawyers who could not fathom that their plan was flawed. To the party institution and the Ottawa political establishment, it was almost inconceivable that an MP, especially a government MP, would dare to vote against his or her own party, but to Paul, it was just something that he had to do.

Chapter 6

Killer Instincts

We hope we elect intelligent, responsible politicians who are freely able to vote for good legislation and against poor legislation. I commend Paul Steckle, and I am proud to have an MP of his calibre to represent our riding. I do not hold the same feeling for the party. I feel that the conduct of our prime minister with regard to the disciplinary measures taken to retard any member from voting or speaking for his or her constituents is an insult to the parliament ... and to the Canadian people.

—R. John Elliott, Blyth
In a letter to *Focus* magazine
April 1995

Wednesday, February 15, 1995, was National Caucus day. As is the tradition, each Wednesday morning during the weeks when Parliament is in session, all Liberal senators and Liberal members of the House of Commons gather in Room 237-C of the Centre Block for what only can be described as a private, closed-door, "family" meeting. Few know what actually takes place in such a meeting, aside from those in attendance, their trusted advisors and most senior staff. While there are leaks to the press from time to time, caucus secrecy is maintained for the most part.

These meetings are one of the few systemically entrenched occasions when the leader of the party sits in front of the caucus and invites both praise and critique. The feedback, which is delivered from the floor, is, in most instances unpolished, direct and blunt. Elected Members of Parliament and their colleagues in the Senate tell the party leader, face-to-face, exactly what is bothering them and how to fix it. Strategy, policy and—on occasion—party discipline are all potential agenda items for the two-hour congregation.

In 1995 there were more than two hundred Liberals clambering to attend National Caucus. Parliament Hill security and RCMP officers were posted at the doors and the national news media was in a frenzy to interview the various elected officials on the previous day's events. Most particularly, the media was on the hunt for the three rookie MPs who publicly opposed their own government the night before on the fundamental issue of gun control.

The three Ontario parliamentarians who defied the orders of the Chief Government Whip and invited the anticipated consequences were Benoît Serre (Timiskaming-French River), Rex Crawford (Kent), and Paul Steckle (Huron-Bruce). They now jointly occupied Mr. Chrétien's black list for their blatant show of defiance. All that remained was doling out the punishment to the offending politicians.

It just happened that Prime Minister Chrétien was in Dallas, Texas, at that time, and the man acting in his stead was the Honourable Herb Gray. Herb, who today is known as the Right Honourable Herbert Eser Gray, PC, CC, QC, BComm, LlB, LlD (Hons.), was first elected to the House of Commons in the southern Ontario riding of Essex West on June 18, 1962. During his nearly 40-year career in Ottawa, he served in a number of high-profile cabinet postings, including Minister of Revenue, Minister of Industry, Minister of Regional Economic Expansion, President of the Treasury Board, Solicitor General of Canada, Minister Responsible for the Millennium Bureau, and Deputy Prime Minister. On this day, February 15, 1995, Herb was the acting prime minister. It was his job to hand out the demerit points and to enforce a code of strict party rule.

It is important to note that while Mr. Gray was and is a very nice person, his ideology is old school. Breaking party solidarity, to Mr. Gray, was unthinkable. While I was not privy to his thoughts on the occasion, I am certain that he desperately wanted to stop backbench MPs from voting in a manner inconsistent with party leadership. He needed to punish the three wrongdoers, while at the same time sending a clear message to the 49 other Liberal MPs who either stayed away from the vote or abstained during the formal voting process. Much also was made of the fact that gun control was a Red Book platform item. That, coupled with the fact that the Liberal caucus numerically dominated the fractured and chaotic Opposition parties in the House, emboldened Mr. Gray with a sense of confidence and partisan obligation. Almost everyone on Parliament Hill believed that the castigation would be immediate and decisive.

Paul's legislative assistant at the time, Sarah Trant, was nearly apoplectic over the entire affair. She even went so far as to secretly contact Paul's wife by telephone, urging her to use her influence with Paul to "talk some sense into him." It was utter desperation, because no one seemed to know how this type of insubordination would be viewed by the Liberal leadership. Most of Paul's family and staff members were more than a little concerned with the potential implications. Not only had this kind of thing never happened before, but the anticipation and the uncertainty of what was to follow was almost too much to bear. Would he be kicked out of the Liberal caucus to sit as an independent? Would he be removed from his committee duties? No one knew for sure, but the gossip was in high gear, and it seemed that there was no stopping it.

Even before he cast his vote against the ill-conceived and much-maligned legislative package, Paul knew that there almost certainly would be a negative impact on his political career. Aside from the fact that he had been directly warned by the Office of the chief government whip and, via the media, by the prime minister himself, Paul had been in politics long enough to know that for every action there was an equal and opposite reaction. On the day following the vote, Paul had an inkling that he and his other "renegade" colleagues would be the topic of heated conversation at National Caucus, so he opted to stay in his legislative office to await the executioner's hand. He didn't regret voting the way he did, nor did he doubt that his actions were in keeping with the majority view of his constituents, but the new MP anticipated that the consequences would be dire.

Little time passed before Paul's phone rang; the verdict was in. The news was relayed by Don Boudria, the Chief Government Whip and future personal friend of Paul's. Paul was judged as guilty of speaking his mind, and the sentence was Paul's immediate removal from his post on the Standing Committee of Agriculture and Agri-Food. The news was out within moments and made its way towards a very angry Canadian public.

Although the decision came to be viewed negatively by the public, in Paul's eyes the "sentence" was much lighter than he originally anticipated. While being removed from the Agriculture Committee and relegated to the Parliamentary Library Committee, a second-tier body of book counters, most certainly was an attempt by the party brass to embarrass Paul, it truthfully constituted the best result that he could have conceived at the time. While he would never freely admit it, I am certain that Paul believed that his days with the Liberal caucus would be curtailed as a result of his actions. That is, when he cast his vote against Bill C-68, Paul believed that his expulsion from the caucus would be the logical outcome. Despite this, he voted with the people of Huron-Bruce, something that clearly was not lost on the voters in the constituency.

The reaction from constituents—and seemingly, Canadians from coast to coast to coast—was almost immediate. An inside source at the Prime Minister's Office (PMO) noted that the PMO received tens of thousands of angry letters and calls over the matter. While hunters and other gun owners were obviously pleased with the actions of the three rebel Liberals, the issue quickly underwent a metamorphosis and escalated into a debate on simple democratic representation. (In the months that followed the actual vote, even the venerable Eugene Whelan, former Trudeau cabinet minister and Liberal leadership contender, stated publicly his disapproval with the punitive actions taken against the trio for doing their duty as representatives of the people). The truth is that most Canadians believed that they elected parliamentarians to be their voice in Ottawa. In January 1993,

Mr. Chrétien (before he was elected prime minister) seemed to identify with that belief when he promised more free votes in the House of Commons. Canadians responded favourably, but with the reprimanded MPs on front pages across the nation, the entire façade seemed to be unravelling.

In Huron-Bruce alone, countless editorials denounced Mr. Chrétien's "autocratic and repressive" approach to government. Many could not believe that their MP was to be punished by the very man who had promised to be open and accountable to the people who elected him. The entire issue of democratic representation seemed to ignite intense and blinding fireworks.

In a *London Free Press* article, Rory Leishman remarked, "Granted, the gun-control legislation is controversial. But that's exactly the kind of issue the Chrétien government vowed it would allow its members to exercise their conscience on … For years, Opposition Liberals railed against the 'arrogant style of leadership' practiced by the Mulroney Conservatives, but what do we find now?"[1] He went on to encourage Serre, Crawford, and Steckle to continue to openly challenge their party in an attempt to be the genuine voice of the people, hence encouraging real, open, and honest debate in the House of Commons.

On the same subject, Morris Della Costa, an editorialist for the *London Free Press* wrote, "[Rex Crawford and] Huron Bruce MP Paul Steckle have proven that just because they are politicians doesn't mean they've lost their ability to make individual decisions … Thank goodness for that. What's unfortunate is that the governing federal Liberals think that individual thinking is dangerous."[2] The critical nature of the commentary continued in the many local papers in Huron-Bruce. With headlines like "Liberal MP goes against the grain for his constituents" and "Must MPs be sheep," there seemed no end to the public outcry and outrage. As a result, the Liberal Party, in general, and Mr. Chrétien, in particular, were mired in

---

1. Rory Leishman, What happened to Liberal free vote promise? (*The London Free Press*), 1995.
2. Morris Dalla Costa, Liberals made a sham of the process (*The London Free Press*), 1995.

unflattering comparisons to certain third-world dictators and historical and/or Communist Party tyrants. At the same time, Paul was garnering the personal support and political standing of a local celebrity or that of a near-martyr in some quarters.

While the opposition to the Liberal gun-control proposals contained within Bill C-68 was not universal, I would say that the vast majority of the Canadian people seemed outraged at the notion that members of Parliament would face partisan sanctions for performing their constitutional duty—that of representing their constituents. Robert Hamather, a Hensall resident, summed it up best when he wrote:

> Dictatorship ... Has the Liberal Party moved to their lowest level? Gun control "yes or no" is not the issue. The true issue is the total disregard by the government for our elected representative Paul Steckle and his ability to carry the message of his riding to the House of Commons in a democratic way. The Liberal Party's most recent actions have shown the party to be guilty as charged (dictatorial) ... The "Gutless Wonders" that won't stand up and vote as their ridings instruct them and won't vote against the party elect to stand behind the curtain without voting at all. The elected such as Mr. Paul Steckle who really represent the riding are penalized for having the guts to do so. It is my contention that the Liberal Party owes Mr. Steckle an apology and reinstatement to his former status.[3]

Under the intense and unflattering spotlight of the media and public backlash, the party establishment, to its credit, relented in just less than 24 hours. In an effort to quell the negativity, Paul and his other "partners in crime" were quietly restored to their previous committee assignments and, in time, the party came to devise a formal system of multi-line whip votes. Perhaps an even more telling example of the Liberal Party's desire for change came in February 2007, when Stéphane Dion, the newly elected Liberal leader, welcomed the formerly Conservative MP for Halton, Ontario, Mr. Garth Turner, into the Liberal fold. Mr. Turner had been

---

3. Robert Hamather, in a letter to the editor of local Huron-Bruce papers (*The Exeter Times Advocate*), 1995.

unceremoniously ejected from the Conservative Party on October 18, 2006, for allegedly violating the secrecy rules of the Conservative Party and for not bowing to the party's most recent policy whims. In essence, Mr. Turner was banished for doing many of the things that Paul Steckle had perpetrated in 1995. In the new Dion era, the Liberal Party widened the tent to make room for Progressive Conservatives who could no longer remain under Mr. Harper's rigid leadership. Furthermore, the Liberal Party was now experienced in the concept of permitting MPs to vote freely, without reprisal, on issues of importance to them. When Mr. Turner was ousted from the Conservative Party, he stated, "I truly believe that most Canadians want members of Parliament to be their independent champions."[4] He later confirmed that, in his opinion, the Liberal Party was prepared to openly accept that policy. Political observers noted that the trend was perhaps a classic example of revolution leading to evolution. The new, more flexible whip system, specifically constructed to permit Liberal MPs to vote against party legislation while at the same time preserving the need for the maintenance of solidarity and confidence in the House, was most certainly a direct result of the actions of Mr. Serre, Mr. Crawford, and Mr. Steckle.

Even today, few issues are brought up with greater frequency and passion than gun control. Despite having four elections since the Third Reading vote on Bill C-68, there is no other single issue that factors so strongly in how people vote. People remember that Paul stood his ground and voted according to the wishes of his constituents, even at the risk of his own career. In return, they have rewarded him with their electoral support.

Support for the gun control bill was far from unanimous among the various political parties in the House of Commons—while his party voted against Bill C-68, the current Conservative Prime Minister voted in favour of the legislation at Second Reading—but the impact that it has had on our political process and institutions has been profound and unmistakable.

---

4. Hon. Garth Turner, PC, MP, in an interview with national media, October 18, 2006.

In the final analysis, the Liberal majority passed the bill, but seven Liberal MPs, all rural, voted against the legislation in the House of Commons. In the Progressive Conservative-dominated Senate of 1995, the debate was no less fractious than it had been in the House, but for reasons escaping logic, the Conservative majority permitted Bill C-68 to pass without substantial amendments.

Today, Bill C-68 is still a hot issue for parliamentarians, and it is still every bit as controversial as it was in 1995. In the Thirty-ninth Parliament, Bill C-21 has continued the ongoing tradition of Conservative and Liberal MPs, working to tinker with the faltering national registration system. Based upon correspondence and feedback received in Paul's offices in Goderich and Ottawa, many private citizens continue to believe that our elected officials (including those within the current Conservative government) continue to expend public dollars haphazardly, and in the process they continue to short-change our nation's police forces and civilian population alike—police, for not having the new resources required to do their jobs as efficiently as possible; and the public, because police forces are not the recipients of the said new resources. That aside, there is a silver lining to the Bill C-68 cloud. Our political parties were forced to change their thinking on party discipline. The Liberal Party of Canada did not crumble because a few MPs voted against the Whip's orders, and the sky did not fall because the vote count was not unanimous. That realization has brought about many changes. Let's hope that common sense continues to leak into the halls on Parliament Hill, and let's all, as private citizens, remember to vote accordingly and expect nothing less from those who seek to represent us at all levels of government.

Chapter 7

Fraying at the Edges

I, and many other long-standing Liberals, meet people every week who express their disappointment with having voted for a 'Liberal' candidate who cares little for party policies responsible for his election.

—John Gates, past president
Huron-Bruce (Federal) Liberal Association
In a letter to the editors of local papers (1996)

Today, in 2007, Paul Steckle is generally well respected by both the party faithful and the general public at large, but in years gone by, he often has drawn fire for occasionally veering from the path of preordained partisan policy. Paul was never viewed as a party insider; he was never the "chosen one," and he has, in fact, ruffled many feathers during his tenure. His direct nature and his propensity for speaking his mind may have forced him a rung or two down the partisan ladder in Ottawa when compared to certain other local Liberal stalwarts. In a world that often speaks in tongues and requires delicate diplomacy, Paul's perceived bull-in-a-china-shop approach has, at times, angered the local Liberal establishment.

Despite his outcast persona, Paul worked for years to attain his 1993 campaign nomination. It was a hard-fought battle, but he was a seasoned politician at the municipal level, and he had a long history within the federal Liberal Party and as a salesman in the region. Unfortunately, while this kind of experience can help to make a good candidate better, it also can attract political baggage—in real terms, enemies who will work to undermine one's efforts on a range of other fronts.

Huron-Bruce is far from a safe Liberal seat. Quite the contrary, the geographic area known today as Huron-Bruce has been federally represented by MPs such as Thomas Farrow, Robert Porter, Edward Lewis, James Patterson, Thomas Chisholm, James Bowman, Andrew Robinson, John Loney, Henry Cargill, George Spotton, Elston Cardiff, Robert McKinley and Murray Cardiff. While each gentleman has served in his own unique manner, collectively, they all share one thing: They were all members of various incarnations of the modern-day Conservative Party of Canada. While there have been a few Liberals intermittently scattered in their midst, for the most part, traditional Conservatism is the order of the day in Huron and Bruce.

Because of the obvious electoral, socio-economic, and demographic realities at play, all of the MPs from the area, even the Liberal ones, tend to lean at least slightly right of centre on the philosophical and political spectrums. While there is most certainly a left-leaning population in Huron-Bruce, those who are successfully elected to federal office are predominantly of the former.

The left-leaning base tends to divide and support either the Liberal Party or the New Democratic Party at the ballot box. This vote-splitting on the left has, of course, permitted the right to dominate the politics of the area and hence promote the election of Conservatives. Accordingly, as Paul began to gain his legs during his first term as the MP for Huron-Bruce, cutting his teeth on issues such as corporal punishment and gun control, some among the local Liberal base became increasingly agitated and concerned that they might have unwittingly elected a wolf in sheep's clothing.

The subsequent clash began as early as the 1993 election, with a nasty split in the ranks of the Huron-Bruce (Federal) Liberal Association's Executive Committee. Some among the group did not want to provide election funding from the partisan coffers to the newly nominated candidate. Fortunately, democracy prevailed, and the rift was suppressed, at least for a time. But with every succeeding social policy debate, the stitches were pulled, and the wound remained open and raw for many years.

For some local Liberals, the drive to publicly express, via the media, their discontent with Paul was overwhelming. Newspapers benefited from the ensuing "dirty laundry," and readers revelled at the headlines of fantastic local Liberal divisions. While Paul attempted to mend as many variances as he could, there was little he could do to counter the negative Liberal reaction to his genuine policy and political positions and values.

It is important to remember that politics is a game of inches and, as the saying goes, all politics are local. To be successful, one must wage countless small battles, with the end game of attaining an overall and more grandiose or specific goal. Along the way, one partners with allies for a time and then moves to create new partnerships and alliances for the next round. People who may unreservedly support efforts on one issue will vehemently and vigorously oppose the next. This is certainly exacerbated when one exists in a partisan, fan-based environment, such as that of an elected official.

This was a lesson that Paul needed to learn early in his first term. It was no secret that the outgoing president of the Huron-Bruce (Federal) Liberal Association opposed Paul's stand on gun control. Mr. John Gates, a lifelong Liberal and Kincardine-area resident, articulated his thoughts clearly and for all to see in the riding media. It was no secret that the households of many of Paul's key supporters were divided along partisan lines. A blue sign and a red sign on the same lawn are common during elections campaigns. Most surprising to Paul were the letters that came in from traditional "Paul supporters," in which voters expressed their displeasure with his aptitude for swimming against the current. In one such letter, a Bayfield man wrote, "I am writing to express my major disappointment in your attack on or lack of support for the leader of the Liberal Party, Prime Minister Chrétien. Your comments as carried today, November 22, by the media do no service to your reputation. Your action in the last week … is not honourable conduct for a Liberal."[1] This happened at the same time as

---

1. A signed, handwritten, constituent letter to Paul Steckle, MP, (the author's name has been omitted from this publication for privacy reasons), dated November 22, 2000—received by Paul Steckle, MP on November 24, 2000.

Paul's overall popularity seemed to increase. Paul grappled with this difficult and paradoxical situation for the entire span of his career.

The difficulty simply is that candidates often are elected based on a sound bite but are then required to govern by textbook. We want our politicians to be Average Joes, but we expect them to have all the answers. We demand that they be human but then punish them for simple follies that we may have ourselves. We like simple "plain speak," but we grow angry when a slip of the tongue occurs. We expect them to be all things to all people, and then we chastise them for being hypocritical.

In the 112-page Liberal Red Book of the 1993 election campaign, nine simple words—"A Liberal government will strengthen our gun control laws"—touched off a multi-billion-dollar legislative chain reaction that continues to this day. Paul, as the local Liberal candidate, endorsed the notion of strengthening gun control laws but did not endorse a national registration system; the concept was not even discussed at the time. The partisan argument that Bill C-68 was somehow cast in stone during the 1993 election campaign for blanket endorsement by the electorate is laughable, at best. Furthermore, in that same Red Book, an explicit promise was made to create an independent ethics councillor who would report directly to Parliament, not to the prime minister. Remember, it was an *explicit* promise; the exact wording being, "A Liberal government will appoint an independent ethics councillor to advise both public officials and lobbyists in the day-to-day application of the Code of Conduct for Public Officials. The ethics councillor will be appointed after consultation with the leaders of all parties in the House of Commons and will report directly to Parliament."

Despite this, the Liberal caucus voted in 2000 against a motion that read:

> That this House adopt the following policy from the Liberal Red Book One and call for its implementation by the government: A Liberal government will appoint an independent ethics councillor to advise both public officials and lobbyists in the day-to-day application of the Code of Conduct for Public Officials. The ethics councillor will be

appointed after consultation with the leaders of all parties in the House of Commons and will report directly to Parliament.

The vote tally, in which the Liberal majority in the House defeated the Red Book promise, was 145 to 122. The only two Liberal MPs who voted in accordance with the explicit Red Book commitment of 1993 were Ivan Grose (Oshawa, Ontario) and Paul Steckle (Huron-Bruce, Ontario).

The point is not to shame the National Caucus but rather to respond directly to critics who chastised Paul for being a "maverick" or for not voting in favour of "party policies responsible for his election." In the instance of the ethics commissioner, 145 Liberal MPs violated a party policy that was, in part, responsible for their election. Moreover, it is important to note that while it was the then Opposition Conservatives who drafted and presented the motion, in the current term of the Harper Conservative government, they have yet to reintroduce the motion.

Early in his career, Paul Steckle decided that the apparent practice of rolling promises was unacceptable. He was determined to vote according to the wishes of his constituents, regardless of the consequences to his own career. He kept his word and cast his vote in favour of the explicit promise that helped to get him elected in 1993. Yes, he has voted against the party leadership on certain other issues, but he has never failed to strive to represent the majority view of his constituents. If Paul Steckle is "un-liberal," then so are the 23 other Liberal MPs who opted to vote against their own government between 1993 and 1997—this is the new reality in Canadian partisan politics.

Chapter 8

Judgement Day

Congratulations! You made it back. Well done!
Guns or no guns … you won! Your friend, Gib

—Honourable Gilbert Parent
Speaker of the Canadian House of Commons
In a note to Paul Steckle (June 17, 1997)

March 19, 1997, was, in many respects, just another day. But in actuality, it was day number one in a drive that would dominate the lives of countless volunteers before federal election day on June 2. It was the day that Paul Steckle was to formally seek the nomination from the Huron-Bruce (Federal) Liberal Association to run for re-election as their candidate in the 36th general election.

Paul's first term in office was a learning experience for everyone involved. He was anything but quiet, as many new backbenchers generally tend to be, and he garnered considerable public and media attention, both good and bad, for his efforts. As a result, he was labelled as a maverick, a title that seemed to be a source of both pride and popularity for him.

Given his profile, his controversial nature, and his proclivity for butting heads with Mr. Chrétien, there was some concern among Paul supporters that the leader of the Liberal Party, who retained veto power on all nominations, would deny Paul the use of the Liberal banner for his re-election campaign. Not only would such a move prevent Paul from accessing any available partisan funding, but it also would deal him a serious blow with respect to any re-election bid. Historically speaking, everyone professes to desire an independent MP between elections, but at election time few seem prepared to vote for an independent candidate. In 1997, there were those involved with the local Liberal association, particularly those opposed to Paul's personal positions on certain contentious issues, who secretly hoped that Mr. Chrétien would step up and rid them of this non-conformist MP who refused to bow to the will of the Chief Government Whip in Ottawa. Either way, as the date of the Huron-Bruce nomination meeting approached, all eyes were on Paul.

When Paul first announced his intention to again seek the Liberal nomination, the media jumped on the story. John Greig of the *Wingham Advance Times* wrote, "One of the federal Liberal party's most controversial members is seeking re-election. Huron-Bruce MP Paul Steckle told a press conference on Friday in Goderich that he is eager to serve for a second term."[1] Despite the hype and the anticipated fallout, when Paul Steckle stood on the platform at the Royal Canadian Legion in Lucknow, the unopposed incumbent not only secured the nomination but also received multiple standing ovations from the Liberals in the crowd.

Paul spoke of Liberal accomplishments, and he spoke to his own record. He spoke of the work not yet finished, and he claimed partial credit for new freedoms that MPs have with respect to whipped votes. All in all, Paul did what he always did: He spoke the truth as he saw it. He was rewarded with the leader's endorsement and with a personal letter from Prime Minister Chrétien, which read:

> I would like to offer heartfelt congratulations on your re-nomination. I am especially pleased and proud because you are a member of the finest team of candidates put together by a federal party in decades; the Liberal class of 1993 … Your hard work and dedication have now been rewarded with a renewed vote of confidence. I look forward to working

---

1. John Greig, Paul Steckle seeks re-election (*The Advance Times*), March 1997.

with you and your campaign team in the coming weeks and months. Together, we will bring about a great national victory, carrying forward one century of achievement and nation-building into the next.[2]

It seemed that Mr. Chrétien's skin was not as thin as some would believe or suggest.

With the nomination process out of the way, the campaign kicked off in earnest. Bob Swartman was the campaign manager, and David Johnston was the local riding association president. Eventually, the team reassembled and the momentum began to build.

It was a very different electoral map this time out. The Progressive Conservative Party was still reeling from their stunning demise in 1993, and the Reform Party, while largely viewed as an exclusively Western and far-right posse, was picking up some wind in their sails. The New Democratic Party (NDP) remained largely in the political wilderness, and the separatist Bloc Québécois had faltered since their surprise attainment of Official Opposition status in the House. All in all, the Liberals, while waning in some regions, seemed poised for a strong second straight victory. The Opposition parties knew this and altered their strategies accordingly. In Huron-Bruce, candidates ran for second place—that is to say that they acknowledged openly that the Liberals would be reelected as the Government of Canada but urged voters to elect an Official Opposition that is loyal to Canada. Similar statements were made by numerous Reform Party sources. Clearly, the strategy was more than a passive attempt to capitalize on the anger that existed locally over the idea that a political party—one openly dedicated to the sovereignty of Quebec—could be sworn in as Her Majesty's Loyal Opposition.

Locally, the Reform Party nominated Doug Fines, a 47-year-old business owner and member of the Goderich Chamber of Commerce and Lions Club, as their standard bearer (This status was solidified only after Paul Steckle declined a request from local Reform Party organizers to abandon the Liberals in favour of a run as the Reform Party candidate).

---

2. Rt. Hon. Jean Chrétien, PC, MP, Prime Minister of Canada, in a letter to Paul Steckle, MP, April 14, 1997.

The NDP nominated the 43-year-old, self-professed (albeit unverified) former Liberal supporter and healthcare worker, Jan Johnstone. Dave Joslin, a 48-year-old dye machine operator, made his debut for the Christian Heritage Party, and Huron County Board of Education trustee and entrepreneur Colleen Schenk lent her name for the consideration of Progressive Conservative voters. The names were now on the ballot; the real race had begun.

In 1997 Canada was still recovering from a massive economic recession. Unemployment, while lower than it was in 1993, still topped 9.5 per cent, and the national debt continued to rise. Aside from economic issues, justice issues continued to dominate the national campaign. To help combat this, Paul Steckle received the formal endorsement of the Canadian Police Association, one of only eight Liberal candidates to receive the nod for a tough-on-crime position (ironic, considering that Paul Steckle voted against Bill C-68). By contrast, then-Justice Minister Alan Rock was openly rebuked by the group for being soft on crime, a move that seemed to act as a catalyst for the continuing deterioration of the tone of the national campaign. Subsequent to that, the Liberal Party set its sights on the Reform Party, seeking to label it as anti-immigration, anti-women, bigoted amateurs who were not worthy of becoming national government. In return the Reformers blasted the Liberals as arrogant, healthcare-cutting nationalists who wanted little more than to have their hands in the pockets of the little guy. Fortunately, the nasty tone largely stayed out of the Huron-Bruce contest, where cordiality reigned.

In the end, after numerous town-hall meetings, endless main-streeting, and a seemingly nonstop barrage of media ads, Paul Steckle and the Liberals were elected, both locally and nationally. While the national margin was smaller than in 1993, of the 301 seats available in the House of Commons, the Liberals secured 155 seats; the Reform Party collected 60; and the BQ, the NDP, and the Progressive Conservatives earned 44, 21 and 20 seats, respectively. There was even one independent MP elected—a rarity in federal politics—in the Toronto riding of York South-Weston (a prominent former Liberal John Nunziata).

In Huron-Bruce, the race was not as close. Incumbent MP Paul Steckle received a huge majority—24,240 votes. Doug Fines acquired 9,925 votes; Colleen Schenk, Jan Johnstone, and David Joslin obtained 9,223 votes, 3,037 votes and 781 votes, respectively.

In his victory speech Paul remarked that his renegade way had provided him with an electoral shot in the arm. In his address to supporters, Paul proudly proclaimed, "I gave the people the representation they were looking for ... The people of this riding want member representation in Ottawa on issues that are important to them, and I will continue with that style of representation ... I made a commitment to speak on behalf of the people, and I think I made decisions that touched the hearts of people."[3]

Election number two was over; the Steckle dynasty seemingly had begun.

---

3. Paul Steckle, MP, in his acceptance speech to Liberal supporters, June 2, 1997.

Chapter 9

Act as if Ye Have Faith and Faith Shall Be Given

Dear Paul; thank you for leading our Prayer Breakfast group last week. I felt it was a very good "lesson," both in content and in the spirit you gave our time together. It was as close as we've come to sharing from our hearts without reservation. It was nice. Following the meeting (actually, it was on the plane trip home) I jotted down this poem, based on what I saw last Wednesday morning. Pulitzer it's not, but heartfelt it is.

The Simple Act of Giving
I met a friend the other day; passed the time with idle chatter
But I listened as he talked of life and what should really matter
He told me of his family, his principles, and love
He said that it's our "simple acts" that show what we are made of.
He wondered if the right stuff would be flowing through his veins
If he had to, would he stand his ground
When it might cause him pain
He thought a bit, and mentioned that he hoped he would be seen
As firm in tribulation as his Mentor once had been
The person that he spoke of gave His life so we could live
And He showed us true compassion as He challenged us to give
His simple Act of Giving crashes o'er me like a flood
Cause his Mentor—our dear Jesus taught us giving by His Blood.

—Honourable Chuck Strahl, PC, MP,
(Conservative) Minister of Agriculture and Agri-Food
In a handwritten note to Paul Steckle

To many casual observers of politics, particularly those who study the daily Question Period in the House of Commons, it may seem that Canada's political parties stand on the constant brink of institutional insurrection. Party leaders violently pound their fists and furrow their brows in a seemingly unending state of total rage with their political opponents. Solemn decorum and ancient formal procedure give way to what appears to be anarchy and near bedlam. Otherwise mature pillars of the community turn the dignified floor of the House of Commons into a setting that could embarrass even the most ill-behaved and roguish pre-schooler. Indeed, the 45-minute daily Question Period has been described both as the best theatre in Ottawa and the worst spectacle on Parliament Hill.

To those who actually participate in the hubbub of Question Period, however—staffer, spin doctor, media personality, or Member of Parliament—Question Period is something quite different. Question Period (not "answer period," as Paul is so fond of quipping) is the time when the major television news networks shift to live coverage of the House of Commons. It is a time when ratings spike, and—most importantly—it is one of the few times when elected politicians get to cut loose and deliver an unfiltered message directly to the Canadian population.

Without question, the time designated for the spectacle has been much maligned by the population from time to time, but there is no arguing that people watch it in ever growing numbers. Much like surreptitiously reading the *National Enquirer* (we would not want anyone to know, but we do scan the tabloid in the checkout line at the grocery store), we watch the Question Period because we simply love the pace and wit. The unscripted repartee and wordplay transform an otherwise dry event into an afternoon soap opera—just what the doctor ordered on a quiet weekday afternoon. It might be said that the House erupts in chaos because people are watching, but people are watching because the House is chaotic.

I would encourage anyone who does not want to learn the truth about Question Period to put this book down, because I am going to let you in on a trade secret. Question Period is closer to theatre than it is to drama. The banter is scripted, researched, vetted, and even rehearsed before it is delivered on the floor of the House. MPs and ministers get together to practice, just to make sure that the indignation looks right or that the exasperation does not go too far for the occasion. Often, the Opposition even tells the government, in advance, which questions it intends to ask, so that proper answers can be prepared. Sure, there are instances when passion makes a brief appearance, but for the most part, even Shakespeare would be proud of our parliamentarians.

This leads me to my point: By and large, Members of Parliament, regardless of their political stripe, are not usually sworn enemies. In fact, in many cases, particularly those of loss or tragedy, members support one and another as would friends, work colleagues, or even close neighbours. Sure, there are certain members who may have personality conflicts, but more often than not, affability permeates the place.

As someone viewing the situation from the inside of the "Hill culture," I have learned over the years that despite the often-repeated and seldom-understood theory that church and state should and must remain separate, it is indeed faith that tends to connect parliamentarians in a way that little else could. Often, there is a kinship between members of which little is spoken outside of Ottawa, an empathy and understanding that runs much deeper than outward partisan divisions. There are most certainly mechanisms that assist with the fostering of this faith-based blending, but I must confess that it is the spontaneous demonstrations that are the most poignant.

One such example would be when Liberal MP Shaughnessy Cohen collapsed one afternoon, without warning, in the House of Commons just after Question Period. Liberal cabinet ministers and MPs from all sides of the House, including Paul Steckle, who was sitting just behind Ms. Cohen when she fell, immediately rushed to her side, smashing out her desk and commencing CPR in an effort to revive her stricken and lifeless body. Those same MPs, who had, only moments earlier, fiercely battled during Question Period, followed the paramedics to the hospital and held a constant vigil over their fallen comrade. They stayed late into the night, disregarding all other commitments, and returned to the House the next day to verbally pay tribute to the life of their colleague and friend. Tears and kind words came from every party, as the flag atop the Peace Tower was brought to half-mast as a mark of profound respect. Such behaviour is what really happens when the cameras are turned off.

Most Canadians might be surprised to learn that former prime minister, the late Pierre Elliott Trudeau, considered his spiritual director a desirable element of his life. Mr. Trudeau had a deep personal spirituality that was a tremendous, albeit private, component of his life and career. Following his example, parliamentarians for generations have embraced a healthy spirituality, and certain institutions of government have evolved to support this. Groups like the Parliamentary Pro-Life Caucus (PPLC), the National Prayer Breakfast, and the All Party Interfaith Committee of the Canadian Parliament (APICCP) have seemingly found a way to set aside partisan and cultural differences in favour of building upon common ground on issues of "absolute truths."

Over the years, Paul Steckle has played an active role in the evolution and advancement of these groups, specifically the National Prayer Breakfast, the weekly Parliamentary Prayer Breakfast and the PPLC. Unlike Mr. Trudeau, Paul's personal faith has never been a guarded secret. He has spoken of it frankly and publicly on many occasions. While this often has proven beneficial, in other instances it has prompted pronounced opposition. I recall instances when constituents, colleagues, and even a United Church minister condemned Paul for publicly professing a belief in God. Enduring name-calling and charges of fanaticism, Paul has persevered because he refuses to accept that our Charter guarantee of freedom of religion is intended to promote a freedom *from* religion. Religion and politics are forever intertwined, as surely as people and politics are entangled, and there is absolutely nothing wrong with that, legally or otherwise.

Paul has chaired both the PPLC and the National Prayer Breakfast during his tenure. In 1998 Paul accepted the position of chair of the annual Canadian National Prayer Breakfast. This group, which is similarly styled to the United States Congressional National Prayer Breakfast, has been in operation for more than 40 years. Its mandate is simple. It "brings together responsible leaders in a spirit of meditation and prayer for themselves and for the nation. The Breakfast further serves as a quiet demonstration that men and women in positions of responsibility place a high priority on spiritual values."[1] I was fortunate enough to be Paul's guest at the National Prayer Breakfast in 1999, and I was impressed with the grandness of the guest list—the prime minister of Canada, each of the party leaders, Speakers of the House and Senate, the vast majority of the federal cabinet, Chief Justice of the Supreme Court, the diplomatic corps, countless members of the Senate and House of Commons, parliamentary staff, and numerous members of the public. Imagine, the Who's Who of official Ottawa, breaking bread with each other and with average citizens, for the express purpose of discussing their faith and showing Canadians that it was both an acceptable and highly desirable undertaking.

As I looked about the room I saw ambassadors and high commissioners from every region of the globe, sitting side by side. I saw the representatives of sworn enemies sharing breakfast and talking about their personal faith—an issue that, in some instances, has divided their people for countless centuries. It was a remarkable and moving sight, one that plays out each and every year on Parliament Hill.

As the chair of that event in 1998, Paul Steckle was responsible for organizing the entire affair. The guest list, the food, the room, the setup, the entertainment, the guest speaker, and the formal program all required his attention, down to the most minute detail. It was executed flawlessly, and the tradition continues to this day.

The Parliamentary Pro-Life Caucus (PPLC) is yet another example of how MPs from all political parties work together to advance issues of personal importance in a faith-based environment. The structure of the group is such that there is a government and an Official Opposition co-chair. Paul, in his current capacity as Liberal co-chair, has worked closely with the group since his election in 1993. The PPLC is made up of several MPs and senators, who share a common pro-life approach to what they call "life issues." These issues include (but are not limited to) abortion, euthanasia, stem-cell research, unborn victims of violence legislation, and the potential medical repercussions of intentional miscarriage. The membership of the

---

1. Canadian National Prayer Breakfast mandate, expressed on the formal event program, April 23, 1998.

group is not for public disclosure, but it can be said that a range of personalities attend, including cabinet ministers, past and present. One of the key rules of the group is that the politics are left at the door. All MPs and senators are welcome, as long as any partisan agenda is left outside. Aside from offering cohesion on issues of mutual concern, the PPLC and other groups like it foster friendships across the political divide.

Despite the fact these groups are much maligned and under almost constant attack and scrutiny for not being politically correct or understated with respect to their faith and personal morality, I would suggest that they serve as essential, if unspoken, non-partisan support network. In my opinion, more inclusive and non-partisan co-operation can only benefit our parliamentary system of governance in general.

Chapter 10

Neither Omnipotent Nor Omnipresent

The biggest surprise of being prime minister is how much time is taken up with foreign affairs. It's enormous. Everything we do now is global. It's just the nature of the world.

—Prime Minister Stephen Harper
In an interview with the *Sun Media* chain
Recounted by Lawrence Martin
In *The Globe and Mail* (November 11, 2006)

When Canadians vote for their local Member of Parliament, I would suggest that very little consideration is given to a candidate's ability to actually function effectively on the world stage. What are the candidate's language abilities? What is the candidate's knowledge of certain foreign cultural sensitivities? Has the candidate any personal history on the international scene? These all are questions that should be posed to any aspiring contender for a seat in Parliament. We Canadians, however, generally select our choice for MP based upon his or her party affiliation, knowledge of local issues, vocational background, ability to charm a crowd, and perhaps even physical appearance. It has been my experience that a foreign-affairs background is one of the least-considered factors during a local election campaign, but it represents one of the single greatest skill sets once an MP is in office.

This is somewhat perplexing, given the evolving and changing nature of our economy and our day-to-day lives in the global context. A range of commonly discussed federal issues—such as agriculture support structures, supply management, trade policy, immigration targets, national defence-spending priorities, domestic security concerns, aviation regulations, civilian travel, banking, healthcare and financial policy—can depend upon the international political climate and the winds of change. Failure to properly manage foreign affairs can have dire repercussion on important domestic policy items. In short, just because a voter fails to take an interest in foreign affairs doesn't mean that foreign affairs won't take an interest in the voter.

To help illustrate the importance of personal skills and relationships in the formation and maintenance of effective foreign policy, I would cite the fact that in 1973 Prime Minister Trudeau, a shrewd and dynamic political force, dined with Chinese Premier Chou En-lai in an effort to open trading opportunities and to address certain humanitarian issues with the gentle hand of a friend. Since that time, most Canadian leaders have appreciated that the largest national population on the planet, China, is of paramount importance to Canada on a range of fronts. There are obvious economic benefits to trading with the Chinese, but there also are other advantages. By contrast, if our government was to isolate or to intentionally embarrass the Chinese government in Beijing by taking an overly aggressive stand on any policy matter, the tactic might nudge the Chinese away from the notion of cooperating with western governments; something that could have calamitous global consequences on health issues (such as SARS) or on matters of global security (such as the North Korean nuclear threat). Indeed, when properly motivated, China generally has been much more cooperative with the West than when cajoled by threats or intimidation. Whether combating human rights violations or seeking to democratize the region, individual MPs have a tremendous role to play in the process.

During his tenure, Paul Steckle has played a quiet but important role on the international scene; he's carried a simple message of the virtue of honest, democratic representation. When he was first elected to the House of Commons on October 25, 1993, he was a neophyte on the international stage, but since then he has made his mark in many regions, most definitively in Asia and Africa.

Paul's first modest dabbling into international relations came on June 28, 1997, at the Royal York in Toronto, when he was invited to participate in the state dinner for Her Majesty Queen Elizabeth II and His Royal Highness the Duke of Edinburgh. While Paul's role in the state dinner was minor in nature, it did open his eyes to the impact that he could have on the global stage, perhaps foreshadowing what was to come. During his first term in office, Paul had given little thought to the possibilities that might emerge on the foreign stage, but a mere 26 days following his re-election in June 1997, his perspective on the matter had changed.

MPs routinely meet and correspond with foreign representatives in Canada to address areas of mutual concern. While there are some instances when government MPs engage in foreign relations during their formative career years, the bulk of the work is left to the more seasoned of their numbers. Standing committee chairs and members with specific experience or knowledge in areas of specialized fields also have a tremendous opportunity to advance national interests and, by default, the interests of their local region. Paul's résumé clearly demonstrates that his specialities range from agriculture and fisheries to spirituality and local governance—all spheres that would present tremendous opportunities in the years between 1998 and 2007.

In 1998 Paul was selected as chair of the Canadian National Prayer Breakfast. The title put him in a position to deal with every member of the Canadian diplomatic corps and placed him on the guest list for the United States Congressional Prayer Breakfast. Not everyone would view this as a prestigious assignment, but it was most certainly an opportunity to engage in diplomacy on an entirely new level.

On December 10, 1997, Paul and Kathy Steckle received an official invitation from U.S. Senator Daniel K. Akaka, the chairman of the Congressional Committee organizing the 46th annual National Prayer Breakfast. Along with members of the U.S. Senate and Congress, President Clinton and the First Lady, Vice President Gore, and a range of government officials, the diplomatic community, and international leaders from more than 160 nations, Paul was invited to participate in the Breakfast and in a long list of peripheral leadership events in early February 1998. This provided him with the opportunity to meet with and discuss numerous cross-border issues with global and U.S. policy makers. Business cards and private meetings flowed freely, and Paul's private Rolodex increased with each egg, slice of bacon, or glass of fresh-squeezed orange juice that appeared on the table. His international debut was nothing short of a complete success.

Some time later, in September 2001, Paul received a call from senior U.S. Congressman Tony Hall, whom he had met at the Prayer Breakfast. The congressman was seeking a posting to lead the United Nations World Food Program. The position had a direct and unmistakable link with Canadian agriculture. Remembering their discussions at the Breakfast and calling upon a budding friendship, the Ohio congressman contacted Paul to ask for an international reference. Paul obliged and, in doing so, secured an advantage with a tremendously influential person in the field of agriculture and agri-business, a relationship that proved fruitful for all concerned, including the constituents of Huron-Bruce in subsequent years.

Given Paul's experience with Her Majesty the Queen and with the U.S. Prayer Breakfast behind him, he turned his attention to the continent of Africa. Although he did not know it at the time, Africa and the extreme poverty endemic to that region would, in time, become an issue close to his heart. The awareness began ambiguously with an invitation to meet with then-President Nelson Mandela of South Africa. President Mandela visited Canada in mid-September 1998, and he later was recognized by the Government of Canada, which bestowed Canadian Citizenship upon him for his heroic efforts to end apartheid in his beleaguered homeland. As Mr. Mandela addressed the Canadian Parliament on the morning of Thursday, September 24, 1998, Paul Steckle watched with interest. The Nobel Prize-winning statesman spoke of the horrors that he and his nation had endured during the long struggle for true democracy. While Paul never called upon Nelson Mandela or any official in Mandela's administration, he drew great strength from the president's personal story and used it as a compass during his visits to Africa in ensuing years.

On September 29, 1998, Paul attended a dinner with the Commonwealth finance ministers. Paul is no economist, but he is a business-minded fiscal conservative. He believes devoutly in the importance of Canada's social programs, such as healthcare, employment insurance, and the Canada Pension Plan, while at the same time realizing that someone must pay for those vital services. In 1998, Canada was still running a deficit, but it was greatly reduced from the days immediately following the collapse of the Kim Campbell Progressive Conservative government. Canada had pulled itself out of the economic muck, and, as a result, there was a road map for the world's largest economies. The Commonwealth finance ministers, having seen Canada's success, were eager to discuss and debate the lessons learned during the struggle to eliminate the deficit. In short, the model used to bring order to the books was premised on the notion that one must foster growth and prosperity but still live within one's means. The meeting of the Commonwealth finance ministers seemed to complement the sentiments expressed by President Mandela earlier in the week—pay the bills, plan for the future, and protect the vulnerable. This message resonated with Paul in a way that helped to shape his approach to foreign affairs for years to come.

Paul didn't have to wait long to use his "lessons learned" in a practical setting. On Saturday, October 17, 1998, he was invited to address the Pretoria Executive Group, an invitation he happily accepted. The Pretoria Executive Group is a collective of South African business executives who, in their words, "seek to make a lasting difference in the world. Not only are they committed to excellence and success in business but also to productive change in people's lives."[1] The group invited Paul to speak at the Pretoria Country Club in Waterkloof, through the Christian Embassy of

---

1. The Pretoria Executive Group mandate, expressed on an invitation issued to Paul Steckle, MP, October 17, 1998.

Canada and the Christian Embassy of South Africa, two groups that have dedicated themselves to the encouragement of the "political, diplomatic, and executive communities through networking key influencers, sharing principles of leadership that help build [a successful and prosperous nation] ..." Paul's experience in local government, in business, and in national governance was of interest to the executives, given the state of their economy and their efforts to turn the tide. Paul travelled to the region and saw firsthand both the splendour and the hardships faced each day by the local population. He also was given the opportunity to encourage local business leaders to make every effort to help improve the plight of their countrymen.

Up to this point a large portion of his foreign affairs experience focused on creating contacts, learning the ropes, and advocating for better social conditions. On the global stage, Paul was no longer a greenhorn, but he was far from a seasoned or expert veteran. It was in this developmental stage that Paul was presented with a massive opportunity; if realized, it would provide unprecedented economic growth potential for the Bruce County portion of his constituency—it was ITER.

ITER, or the International Thermonuclear Experimental Reactor, was a concept that had been hatched some years earlier. It was a multi-national, multi-year, multi-billion-dollar mega-project that was premised upon a theoretical science and the hope of a nearly inexhaustible source of clear and inexpensive power. The concept is simply explained, but from a scientific perspective it was anything but simplistic. In conventional nuclear reactors, when one atom splits it causes a chain reaction—another atom and another and another subsequently follow suit. And each time an atom is split, a burst of heat is created and released. When enough heat is produced, water is boiled; the resulting steam can move turbines, thus creating electricity for home and business owners. The ITER model is similar, save for one key difference. In the ITER "Tomahawk" reactor, atoms would not be split and a chain reaction would not be initiated. Instead, atoms were to be fused back together, which would prompt heat that far exceeded the temperature of our sun. The lack of a chain reaction would negate the potential for a nuclear meltdown, and the ITER process would consume tritium, a material that is a waste product from conventional reactors. The end result would be massive amounts of power, cheaply produced, with less waste and no chance of meltdown.

From the beginning Paul fought to convince the Government of Canada to buy into the notion of the ITER process. The government was reluctant given that the science was purely theoretical and the proposed reactor was intended for scientific rather than commercial purposes. Indeed, ITER's creators had intended for the project to pioneer the science, not set up retail shop. Either way, it was the mid-1990s answer to a looming energy crisis. In a meeting with then-Industry Minister John Manly and Minister of the Environment Anne McLellan, Paul forcefully and cogently argued on behalf of the project. In the end, the threat of cost overruns and uncertainties with respect to labour and materials sourcing sent the Treasury Board scurrying for the bushes. The Government of Canada wanted nothing to do with costly mega-projects. Paul was not dissuaded; he pressed on, internationally and domestically, to see the project move ahead. In December 1998, Paul attended meetings in Rome as part of the ITER Canada delegation. His primary focus was twofold: to see that ITER became a reality in Canada and to see that Bruce County was the location of the ITER site.

In the end, despite fierce international negotiations, the proposed Bruce site was rejected and Clarington (near Toronto) was given the nod. Ultimately, however, all was for naught—the Russian government funding for the project evaporated, and the project itself collapsed under its own cost projections.

The loss of the ITER initiative was a bitter pill, but it did not prevent Paul from continuing to look abroad for opportunities and solutions to problems facing Huron-Bruce. In February 1999, Paul was part of a multi-partisan Canadian delegation to visit with the U.S. House of Representatives Committee on Agriculture. Agriculture always has been one of Paul's first priorities. The sector supports the entire economy of his exclusively rural riding and is, overall, a massive business. With the approach of the World Trade Organization (WTO) talks—international trade discussions that are of particular interest in Huron-Bruce given their potential impact on the agricultural sectors—Paul and other members of the House of Commons Standing Committee on Agriculture and Agri-Food thought it prudent to meet with their U.S. counterparts to discuss issues of mutual concern. The exchange was useful for all involved, and Congressman Larry Combest of Texas, the committee chair, later referred to it as "frank and open." Without question, Paul was gathering an international reputation as a knowledgeable straight-shooter wherever he went. This reputation became so well known that between September 10 and September 14, 2003, Paul was a Government of Canada delegate to the World Trade Organization Fifth Ministerial Conference in Cancun, Mexico. As part of the Canadian delegation, Paul was specifically tasked with defending the interests of Canadian agriculture. There, in oppressively hot weather, with battleships in the harbour and heavily armed security and police around every corner, Paul entered the big leagues of international trading politics. Industry and governments from around the world were present, each seeking to preserve their own piece of the global economic pie. While the WTO talks eventually failed, much ground was held by Canada, and Paul Steckle was an important part of that success.

Paul has gained a tremendous reputation on the international stage, whether he's pressing for increased funding for Great Lakes Fishery Commission; meeting with high-ranking government officials in Uganda; discussing human rights matters with the deputy speaker of the British House of Lords; shaking hands with the Prince of Wales; calling upon the Japanese government to open borders to Canadian beef; debating electoral reform with the Dutch ambassador to Canada; exploring government structures in Taiwan; arguing the merits of supply management with the Australian ambassador to Canada; or making a formal presentation on the merits of democracy to the People's Republic of China.

Chapter 11

Until You Are Dead

The sentence of this court upon you is that you be taken from here to the place from whence you came and there be kept in close confinement until Tuesday, the eighth day of December 1959, and upon that day and date, you be taken to the place of execution and that you there be hanged by the neck until you are dead. And may the Lord have mercy upon you soul.

—Justice Ronald Ferguson
In sentencing Steven Truscott
Tuesday, September 29, 1959

It was late in the afternoon when the news crackled across the airwaves and into the history books. Seventeen-year-old Paul Steckle sat in his Stanley Township home and listened intently as a young boy—someone younger than Paul—was sentenced to hang for the brutal rape and murder of his 12-year-old female schoolmate, Lynne Harper, whose lifeless body had been found in a wooded area outside of Clinton.

Like many people across the County of Huron, Paul followed the news reports of the grizzly summertime discovery and subsequent events. As he listened to the radio news, Paul attempted to unravel and understand the shocking details of a crime that seemed to steal the innocence of the sleepy farming communities surrounding Air Force Base (RCAF) Clinton. Although Paul did not know Steven Truscott—the 14-year-old convicted of the crime—he was surprised by the rapid nature of the investigation and concerned with the manner in which certain "facts" had been gathered or discounted.

While many of the residents of the county were relieved to know that the young deviant responsible for the atrocity would be punished, Paul couldn't shake the feeling that a terrible mistake had been made. For everyone except the people directly involved, the story soon faded from public view, save for an occasional headline as the entire matter snaked its way through the legal process. Paul, his siblings, and their parents continued with their routine, and life returned to normal. In the years that followed, however, Paul considered the fate of the young Steven Truscott on occasion, even though he was not in a position to act on his misgivings about the investigation, the verdict and the sentence.

All that changed on October 25, 1993, when Paul was elected to the Parliament of Canada. While the Truscott case did not jump immediately to mind, Paul was now in a better position to secure answers to the questions that had troubled him for more than three decades. He did not know it at the time, but he was to have an important role in the Truscott file.

In the early 1990s, the Canadian justice system faced a series of high-profile exoneration claims—with the help of new technologies such as DNA testing, many convicted Canadians found themselves absolved of the crimes for which they had been incarcerated. Suddenly, names such as Guy Paul Morin and David Milgaard—both men were falsely convicted, punished and subsequently exonerated—made national headlines as horrific examples of a justice system gone wrong. It was just a matter of time before Steven Truscott's name surfaced again, but this time, Paul was in a position to lend a hand.

Some of Paul's closest advisors and friends were not certain that wading into a 40-year-old murder case, especially to defend the convicted murderer, was a prudent course of political action. But the opportunity was now, and Paul was not prepared to let it pass by.

The Truscott family had engaged the services of AIDWYC, the Association in Defence of the Wrongly Convicted. AIDWYC is a Canadian volunteer organization dedicated to preventing and rectifying wrongful convictions. It had dealt with a number of high-profile matters (Gary Staples, Thomas Sophonow and Benoit Proulx) and the Truscott family was confident that AIDWYC could help ensure Steven's vindication. As the project gathered steam, the Truscott family wisely sought political allies in Ottawa. One of their first contacts was Paul Steckle, Member of Parliament for the area in which Lynne Harper had been murdered. Meetings were held, and Paul readily agreed to do whatever he could to help advance the Truscott family's call for justice. Given Paul's personal history and knowledge of the case details, he didn't need to waste time with research. He simply hurdled himself headlong into the escalating exoneration efforts.

In the spring of 2002, as just one step along the path to Steven's vindication, Paul and his colleague, the Honourable Brenda Chamberlain—Member of Parliament for Guelph, the area in which the Truscott family was residing—began the process of setting up a parliamentary coalition of Truscott supporters, a group that eventually grew to more than 50 Members of Parliament and senators. The sole purpose of the group was to support Steven Truscott in his fight for justice and to keep pressure on the justice minister and Justice Department officials. As Paul suggested, "If we are to keep this issue in the news, we need as many Parliamentarians on our side as possible."[1] And keep it in the news they did. Together, the coalition collected and presented thousands of signed petitions from Canadians who believed that Truscott was innocent.

On February 5, 2003, Paul Steckle presented a Truscott petition to the House of Commons with the following words:

> I rise on behalf of many constituents and petitioners who have submitted their names on paper … The petitioners are calling upon Parliament to ask the minister of justice … to review the case of Mr.

---

1. Paul Steckle, MP, during a telephone interview with David Emslie (*The Clinton News Record*), July 2, 2002.

Truscott. This terrible miscarriage of justice occurred within my riding boundaries. I stand with the petitioners in support of this issue this afternoon, and I, on their behalf, submit these names to Parliament today.[2]

Paul spoke almost daily to the attorney general of Canada about the file. He even loaned consecutive justice ministers his signed copy of the Julian Sher book, *Until You Are Dead*, a book that detailed the oddities of the Truscott case from the beginning, and cajoled them to read it. He twisted the arms and pounded the desks of nearly every elected and non-elected official alike. Paul's effort took on the appearance of a personal crusade.

Paul, Steven and Marlene Truscott (Marlene is Steven Truscott's wife), and a range of other supporters met regularly to discuss details and to gather support to keep up the fight. Their dynamic little group soon grew to a formidable international force; "Justice delayed is justice denied" was their battle cry.

Finally, after considerable effort, on the morning of October 28, 2004, following the formal legal submission for ministerial review from the Truscott legal team, Federal Justice Minister Irwin Cotler agreed that Truscott had "likely suffered a miscarriage of justice" and referred his case to the Ontario Court of Appeal for exploration and examination.

As those words were spoken, Paul Steckle, who witnessed the minister's press conference from the front row of the National Press Theatre, grinned slightly and said, "Now the real work begins." I am not certain Paul fully absorbed the gravity of what had just happened, but I do know that he thought of that summer day, some 45 years earlier, when he first heard the name of Steven Truscott. The helplessness that Paul had felt as a young teen now was replaced by a brief flash of pride at the idea that he had made a small difference in Truscott's life.

Following the minister's press conference, Paul addressed the media:

---

2. Paul Steckle, MP, during the formal presentation of a petition to the House of Commons, February 5, 2003.

Since I was a very young man, I have followed this case. Today, for the first time in many years, I believe that we are moving down the road towards correcting a past miscarriage of justice, finally ridding our justice system of a suspicious cloud that has hung over it for far too long … While I would have clearly preferred an immediate determination of guilt or innocence, I understand and accept the minister's reasons for referring this matter to the Ontario Court of Appeal. I also understand that, while I have clearly indicated my position on this matter in the past, I must refrain from commenting on the validity of any evidentiary items. That charge is now one that belongs to the court and not to politicians … I would like to take a moment to extend my thoughts to the Harper family. This process has unquestionably reopened old wounds, and I would hope that the Ontario Court of Appeal would consider this matter as expeditiously as possible. A quick and thorough decision is, without doubt, in the best interest of Mr. Truscott and the Harper families."[3]

Within minutes of issuing that statement, the calls began pouring in. Steven Truscott again was front-page news in Huron-Bruce and across Canada. Local media rang out with headlines such as "MP to push Truscott appeal" and "Truscott must wait longer" and "Justice delayed for Truscott." Paul's feelings on the Truscott case were well known in the riding, but because there was little understanding of the legal process, people were angry. Again, the chant "Justice delayed is justice denied" began to grow in intensity.

Following the legal referral, the battleground shifted to Queen's Park in Toronto. In an effort to do whatever he could, Paul decided to bring pressure to bear on the Ontario attorney general. On July 28, 2005, Paul issued the following letter to then-minister Michael Bryant.

Dear Mr. Bryant:

I am writing so that I might add my name to the list of those who continue to call upon you to expediently move to rectify the tremen-

---

3. Paul Steckle, MP, during an impromptu scrum with national media outside the National Press Club in Ottawa, October 28, 2004.

dous injustice perpetrated by our justice system upon Mr. Steven Truscott. Today, after nearly half a century of sustained injustice, you have the chance to set things right. Indeed, it is my belief that the verdict in the Truscott case stripped a community of its innocence, robbed a young man of his youth, and permitted Lynne Harper's murderer to go free. With that in mind, I would call upon you to utilize the authority of your office to ensure that the Truscott family can move out from under the cloud of suspicion that has enveloped them for 46 years.

I can vividly remember that summer afternoon in 1959 when I, as a young man, listened on the radio as a judge in Goderich pronounced sentence on the 14-year-old Steven Truscott. "Steven Murray Truscott, I have no alternative but to pass the following sentence upon you … you be taken to the place of execution and that you there be hanged by the neck until you are dead." These are words that have been forever seared into my mind. As the years went on, people in the communities around Clinton began to talk about the odd inconsistencies of the case. As time passed, their questions begat other questions, and substantive answers seemed nonexistent. The lore transferred from generation to generation, and the said peculiarities intensified. In short, from the beginning, few locals, including those close to the case, believed that Steven could have perpetrated the crime that [was] attributed to him. More conspicuously, the authorities seemed impotent with respect to providing accurate and factual explanations.

As you know, after much sustained public and media attention, this matter has again been ignited. Notwithstanding facts such as critical DNA evidence being lost or destroyed by the Crown or testimony of eye witnesses being discounted, the inconsistencies of the case persist. Furthermore, in the past 10 years alone, considerable information has entered into the public domain, underscoring the notion that Mr. Truscott was wrongfully convicted. With that, after considerable judicial research and exploration, Minister Cotler concluded that there was reason to believe that a serious miscarriage of justice occurred in this matter. In essence, the minister acknowledged that the Truscott case is a matter that has sullied the reputation of our justice system for many years and must be resolved. Both on a personal level and as the MP for Huron-Bruce (the place that this all began), I believe that the issue must be resolved conclusively and promptly. While it is not for me to declare guilt or innocence, I do believe that based upon the evidence, a conviction could not be secured today. Accordingly, I believe that it is essential that you recognize this reality and act accordingly.

Minister, I appeal to your sense of fairness when I ask for your personal and immediate intervention to set right the past mistakes of our justice system. Look at the evidence objectively, ask the pointed questions, and then take the appropriate steps. Mr. Truscott has waited for justice for too long.[4]

The letter eventually found its way into the public domain and, while Michael Bryant probably didn't appreciate that kind of attention, Truscott supporters did. Paul's offices in Goderich and Ottawa received several letters of thanks and encouragement from constituents and from concerned Canadians from across the country. As just one example, the following is a letter from a former Huron County resident, who happens to be one of Steven Truscott's elementary school teachers:

Congratulations for writing such an influential letter on behalf of Steve to Attorney General Bryant. I strongly agree with your comments at your "party" that we all must get on the publicity road and show our support for Steve in all the corners that we consider important. Also thanks must go to you and yours for a truly fantastic gathering for all the immediate supporters of Steve and Marlene.[5]

From that July day until January 31, 2007, the Truscott case seemed to languish before the legal system—and then the Ontario Court of Appeal began formally hearing the case, under the watchful eye of the Canadian public, who were permitted to follow the proceedings via television broadcast. While this was the first time that television cameras were permitted in an Ontario courtroom, the move allowed thousands to look in on the progress and the legal and historical arguments made before the five-judge panel. During the opening days of the case, Truscott lawyer James Lockyer spoke passionately and definitively about his client's innocence. He

---

4. Paul Steckle, MP, in a letter to MPP Michael Bryant, Attorney General of Ontario, (provided to the author by Paul Steckle, MP), July 28, 2005.
5. An e-mail received by the office of Paul Steckle, MP, from a former Truscott teacher (the author's name has been omitted from this publication for privacy reasons), received August 7, 2005.

pointed out that crucial evidence had been suppressed or hidden from the original defence team. He drew comparisons between the Truscott, Coffin, and Milgaard cases, and he underscored that the 1999 phase of the Truscott investigation had been the first archival investigation in the history of the Province of Ontario. On the opening day of the hearings, Paul Steckle again rose in the House of Commons, the only member to do so, and again threw caution to the wind as he delivered the following speech:

> On September 19, 1959, in the Goderich, Ontario, courthouse, Justice Ferguson sentenced Steven Truscott to death. On that day nearly 50 years ago, a child's innocence was stolen and a cloud settled over the Canadian justice system that remains still. I can remember as I listened live to the sentence. In the years that followed, my belief that a miscarriage of justice had occurred grew in leaps and bounds. Public concerns grew equally until finally, on October 28 of 2004, the Liberal justice minister said that there [was] reason to believe that a miscarriage of justice may have occurred. With this, he referred the matter to the Ontario Court of Appeal. Earlier today, on live national television, the Court began the process of hearing this matter. I am optimistic that the five justices considering the case will see that there is indeed reason to believe that Mr. Truscott was wrongfully convicted. I wish Mr. Truscott and his family well as they enter into this process, and I look forward to the day when Steven can wake up, for the first time in half a century, an innocent man.[6]

Again, the Truscott case was making headlines and history. While the political and media attention had vacillated over the years, the importance of vindication had never left Paul's radar screen. Paul was quoted in one specific local media article as having said, "My work won't be finished until the day he is exonerated."[7]

Although Steven Truscott has not yet received his justice, the journey has begun in earnest. Paul Steckle fought for and would have preferred a

---

6. Paul Steckle, MP, during a presentation in the House of Commons, January 31, 2007.
7. Jane Sims, MP to push Truscott appeal (*The London Free Press*) November 2004.

more expeditious acquittal, but as the saying goes, politics is a game of inches. Paul remains committed to the cause and is dogged in his belief in Steven's innocence. For now, he draws heartiness from sincere correspondence, such as the e-mail below:

> I am writing to you with the most sincere thank you I can give for speaking out for my father's case. It seems these days that a lot of politicians are only out for themselves and how it may affect their career if they open their mouths and stand up for something they believe in. I applaud you and your courage to do what some are not willing to risk. Thank you again from the bottom of my heart.[8]
>
> Lesley (Truscott) Benson, Kitchener, Ontario

After all, the fight for the downtrodden is what Paul Steckle is all about.

---

8. Lesley Benson, in an e-mail to Paul Steckle, MP, received August 9, 2005.

Chapter 12

Seven Months and Seven Days

I guess when you find yourself after 10 years, and you see new people coming in, and these people find themselves in the inner circle immediately, you have to ask yourself [why] ... I don't know the reasons for doing this, but I do know that [there are] people with expertise in fields that they're not representing in Cabinet, so I guess that's why I'm not the prime minister.

—Paul Steckle, MP
In an interview with Matt Shurrie (the *Goderich Signal Star*)
Commenting on the Scott Brison defection to the Liberal Party
and subsequent appointment to Cabinet

The final months, weeks, and days of Jean Chrétien's tenure as prime minister of Canada were marred by bitter infighting between the Chrétien and Martin factions of the Liberal Party. The tension between Jean Chrétien and Paul Martin first emerged in 1990, when both men campaigned aggressively for the Liberal Party leadership. After a tight, divisive, and often bitter contest, Chrétien defeated Martin and went on to become Canada's prime minister in 1993. In an attempt to manage the obvious and anticipated leadership fallout, Prime Minister Chrétien appointed Paul Martin to the prominent post of Finance Minister. While rumours would suggest that Mr. Martin would have preferred other postings, such as Industry Minister, few would quarrel with the notion that Paul Martin went on to become one of the most prominent and successful finance ministers in Canadian history. Moreover, given the political agenda and economic climate of the day, the finance portfolio arguably went on to become the most influential second-tier position in the federal cabinet. While Mr. Chrétien's leadership style provided all of his cabinet ministers with considerable autonomy relative to their respective portfolios, ambition and pride continued to permeate nearly every element of the personal and private working relationship of the two titans of the Liberal Party. They were a dynamic and effective team, dedicated to working closely to solve Canada's national woes, but behind closed doors, Mr. Chrétien and Mr. Martin were most certainly adversarial competitors, perpetually fighting the 1990 Liberal leadership battle for their place in history.

On June 2, 2002, after years of ministerial continuity in the Finance Department, Prime Minister Chrétien made a sudden and major cabinet change, replacing Paul Martin with Ottawa-South MP and long-time friend and loyalist, John Manley. Prime Minister Chrétien offered countless reasons for the ouster, but nearly everyone in the country was certain that the replacement was directly and inextricably linked to Martin's ongoing campaign to become the next Liberal Party leader. In an effort to keep the mess off of the front pages of the national newspapers, Martin asserted that his conflict with Prime Minister Chrétien was related to a difference in government policy. The forced departure of Paul Martin acted like explosive battery acid—it ignited a civil war within the party that publicly exposed deep divisions within the Liberal establishment between Martin and Chrétien supporters. With the firing serving as a starter's pistol, Martin supporters within the caucus and the Liberal Party began publicly pushing for Prime Minister Chrétien's resignation and the election of Martin as party leader.

The feud continued to intensify until on August 21, 2002, at a summer caucus meeting in Chicoutimi, Quebec, Prime Minister Chrétien surprised Canadians when he announced that he would not seek a fourth term and that he would step down as prime minister, effective on February 1, 2004. Despite the tears and outcries of his supporters, his course was established, and his exit strategy was set in motion. Among other things, the announcement was intended to quell the unconcealed dissent swirling within the Liberal Party and to sidestep the constitutionally required membership review of the party leader's performance, which was expected during the party's next biennial convention. The decision was viewed, in large part, as the result of the serious divisions within the Liberal Party following Paul Martin's departure as Finance Minister. This rift not only threatened Chrétien's continued leadership but also the party's popularity and its ability to continue to govern. Without question, these tensions would have boiled over at the party's convention and leadership review in February 2003, had Mr. Chrétien not taken the actions he did.

While some may have anticipated that the public announcement of Mr. Chrétien's retirement would put down the figurative coup d'état, Martin's supporters regarded the retirement declaration as a sign of weakness and continued to openly rebel and challenge Chrétien's leadership. Policy items in the House suddenly became hotly contested within the Liberal caucus itself. It seemed as though the "Martin administration" was, in some respects, seeking to implement its program in advance of formally receiving the keys to 24 Sussex Drive. In one such example, a motion was passed in the House of Commons in November 2002 to allow the election of parliamentary committee chairs and vice chairs by secret ballot. The Opposition parties and 56 Liberal Members of Parliament, primarily backbenchers (including Paul Steckle), supported the procedural change; Prime Minister Jean Chrétien and his supporters did not. The loss was clearly a personal embarrassment to the 40-year veteran of the House of Commons and seemingly served to detonate a craving for revenge deep within Mr. Chrétien. The Chrétien/Martin quarrel was far from over.

Under a cloud of omnipresent pressure focused on Mr. Chrétien, Paul Martin was elected leader of the Liberal Party of Canada on November 14, 2003. The convention might be described as a coronation rather than an actual contest. The election of Paul Martin was little more than a formality, given that most of the other candidates had withdrawn from the race. With only Heritage Minister Sheila Copps remaining on the ticket, Paul Martin was elected on the first ballot as the leader of the Liberal Party of Canada.

Subsequent to that, Prime Minister Chrétien announced that he would retire from public office on December 12, 2003, clearing the way for Martin to formally and finally become the 21st prime minister of Canada. Liberals everywhere breathed a sigh of relief as, after more than a decade of partisan civil war stemming from the 1990 leadership convention, Paul Martin ascended to the highest office in the land. The collateral damage had been extensive—it arguably is responsible for the eventual decline of the Martin government and the election of the Harper Conservatives in January 2006—but at the time, the hope was that the war was finally over.

There also was a local facet to the story; despite the fact that Paul Steckle had been a leadership campaign worker for Jean Chrétien in 1990, he became a devout Paul Martin supporter over time. Paul Steckle, prodded by a public din within Huron-Bruce, was one of the first Liberal caucus members to publicly call for Mr. Chrétien's retirement, something that happened only after considerable effort had been privately expended. Paul firmly believed that Prime Minister Chrétien had done a spectacular job in the top spot, but he also believed that an effective exit strategy was as important as leadership itself. When he described Mr. Chrétien as "a great prime minister,"[1] he truly meant it. That said, Paul Steckle also recognized that the people of Huron-Bruce wanted change at the top, and if the Liberal Party was not prepared to offer change, the electorate would either force it or find it elsewhere. As a soldier on the front line, Paul could not willingly permit that to happen.

The people of Huron-Bruce took note as Paul Steckle campaigned to promote the merits of the Paul Martin way of doing things. There was a belief among the constituency that once Paul Martin became prime minister, Paul Steckle was set for a big promotion. After all, everyone knew that politicians repaid their friends with favours, right? Moreover, Paul already had been the benefactor of the rise of the Team Martin when he secured the posting of chair of the Standing Committee on Agriculture and Agri-Food. Paul Steckle had been unanimously elected to that post on

---

1. Matt Shurrie, Steckle softening stance on Chrétien retirement (*The Goderich Signal Star*), 2002.

February 4, 2003, after the position was vacated due to the promotion of his predecessor. Most people, however, did not know that earlier that same morning, Paul and all of the Liberal members of the Standing Committee were called to a "family meeting" with the chief government whip. It seemed that the freshman Nova Scotia Member of Parliament, Mark Eyking, was the establishment's favoured candidate for the big chair on the committee. Under the new rules that had been adopted for electing committee chairs by secret ballot, the party leaders could no longer guarantee who would become chair, but that was not going to stop Eyking from trying. In that instance, Paul simply said no. He made it clear that, while he had nothing against Mark Eyking, it was his intention to seek the chairmanship, regardless. "Let the best man win," Paul said, and when the vote was called, Paul Steckle was the only contestant on the ticket. He had his promotion; he had fought for it.

It might have looked as though Paul was on his way up. He was a senior member of the governing party in the House of Commons; he was an aggressive and effective Chair of a prominent Standing Committee; and he was a long-time loyalist and close friend of the heir-apparent to Prime Minister Chrétien. The next logical step was Minister of Agriculture—or so the general public and the media in Huron-Bruce surmised.

When the fateful day for Paul Martin's first cabinet line-up arrived, headlines such as "Maverick MP to get big post," "Bruce County OFA wants Steckle to be next Ag Minister," and "Steckle touted for ag minister" gave way to media banners that read "Steckle could have been a powerful voice," "Condolences to Huron-Bruce voters," and "Steckle shut out." Indeed, Paul Steckle was again locked out of the inner circle. Pundits and reporters postulated as to why, but most agreed with the words of one editorialist:

> Huron-Bruce MP Paul Steckle, a long-time supporter of Prime Minister Paul Martin, missed a shot at becoming Canada's Agriculture Minister because of his reluctance to walk the party line. As chair of the Standing Committee on Agriculture and as a loyal Martin defender, Steckle was well-positioned to take on the important job. He could have been a powerful voice for an industry that's under fire. He did not get the job. Why? Because he didn't want to put himself in an ideolog-

ical straightjacket. He didn't want the job if it meant he had to vote for his party, no matter what. One could argue that an agricultural industry desperately in need of a strong voice will lose out because Steckle's voice was perceived as a little too strong. Steckle's supporters might call him a maverick, and his detractors might call him a loose cannon. There is no question that by "sticking to his guns" and voting against his party many times—and insisting he would do it again—he has denied this country someone who would have made an excellent Agriculture Minister.[2]

To those of us on the inside, there was never any real suspense relating to Paul's prospect of being named to cabinet. We fully expected that Paul would be passed over the first time around. While there was hope for a parliamentary secretary position, a full cabinet seat was never really in the cards. While Paul knew in his head that he was unlikely to make the front benches, I am not convinced that his heart was as certain. He had worked hard to support Mr. Martin, and he'd worked diligently as the chair of the Standing Committee. What else could he do to prove his worth? Paul was genuinely flattered by the media speculation that he was cabinet material, but on that fateful day, December 12, 2003, the day of Paul Martin's first cabinet announcement, Paul's heart was jolted to reality when Bob Speller, Member of Parliament for the Central-Ontario riding of Haldimand-Norfolk, was sworn in as Minister of Agriculture and Agri-Food.

Paul was certainly disappointed, but it quickly became apparent that being excluded from Cabinet may well have been a blessing in disguise. In the few months following Mr. Speller's appointment, the department was rocked by another confirmed case of mad cow disease (bovine spongiform encephalopathy, or BSE) in a Canadian herd. The ensuing fallout, both economically and politically, ravaged the fledgling Martin government. That, combined with the looming sponsorship scandal, eventually led to the general election of 2004, a contest that saw Bob Speller defeated—after just seven months and seven days as Minister—in a wave of voter

---

2. An unsigned editorial, provided by Paul Steckle, MP, that appeared in Huron-Bruce print media (exact date and publication name are unavailable), 2004.

anger that foreshadowed what was yet to come. It is worth mentioning that Mr. Speller's successor, Andy Mitchell, was likewise defeated in the election of 2006, just six short months after assuming the ill-fated posting.

Unlike Mr. Mitchell and Mr. Speller, Paul Steckle went on to win the elections of 2004 and 2006, although the contest in 2006 was considerably closer than projected. During that time, Paul served as the chair of the Standing Committee on Agriculture and Agri-Food, a position that he held until the Liberal Party was reduced to Official Opposition status in the general election of 2006. His chairmanship was vigorous and challenging; especially considering the ongoing demands of the BSE crisis and the farm-income crisis in the grains and oilseed sectors. But Paul was determined to make a difference to the farmers in Huron-Bruce and across Canada. So deep was his dedication to the cause that on Thursday, September 22, 2005, when he received an early morning telephone call from Michelle Cadario, the Prime Minister's Deputy Chief of Staff, inviting him to be sworn to the Privy Council of Canada as Parliamentary Secretary to the Minister Responsible for Infrastructure, Paul respectfully but immediately declined. His rationale was that he could not leave his work on the Standing Committee for reasons of vanity and a pay raise. He would stand by his constituents, even if it meant that he would never sit at the federal cabinet table.

I know that Paul regretted having to make that choice, but I also know that given the same set of circumstances, he would make the same choice again. He has been an elected politician for nearly 30 years, and he has never lost an election—there must be a reason for that. In my opinion, his secret is his motto, "Priority: the people," and his desire to always lead by example and to live by that statement of belief. Paul has a genuine desire to help others, to be a productive member of his community, and to always take the high road. As Paul says, "For every mile of road there are two miles of ditch … and ditches can get pretty muddy once you fall into them."[3]

---

3. Paul Steckle, MP, in conversation with the author, January 22, 2003.

Chapter 13

A Dangerous Step Up

Now I'm chairing the very committee I was thrown off of back
in 1995.

—Paul Steckle, MP,
Newly elected chair of the Standing Committee on Agriculture
February 2003

Most Canadians feel that politics is a relatively safe profession. With the
exception of an occasional paper cut or a necktie caught in a shredder, the
day-to-day lives of elected officials are not exactly filled with death-defy-
ing, adrenaline-generating acts of daring. In the whole of Canadian history
there has been only one instance of an assassination of a nationally elected
official. It may be somewhat ironic that Thomas D'Arcy McGee, a
pre-Confederation Minister of Agriculture and one of the fathers of our
national union, was shot and killed on April 7, 1868, just a stone's throw
from the Parliament Buildings in Ottawa—it's not ironic because he was
shot close to Parliament but because he was simply doing his job (he was
shot following a passionate speech in the House of Commons), and he was
keenly interested in agriculture—two factors that could mirror the modern-day Paul Steckle.

Although Paul did not follow in McGee's ill-fated footsteps, he did narrowly escape McGee's unfortunate end. On March 4, 2003, the VIP security unit of the Royal Canadian Mounted Police was contacted about a threat received against the life of Paul Daniel Steckle.

On February 4, 2003, Paul was unanimously elected to succeed the New Brunswick Member of Parliament Charlie Hubbard as chair of the Standing Committee on Agriculture and Agri-Food. Charlie, who had served as the Agriculture Committee chair for two years between February 2001 and January 2003, was promoted to Parliamentary Secretary to the Minister of Indian Affairs and Northern Development. Paul seemed a natural to fill Charlie's old role and a logical fit for the job. As a pork farmer, a former farm-machinery salesman, and a senior, rurally based Member of Parliament, Paul's qualifications were more than ample. Paul had sought the position in the past and had been passed over for the job, but with a change to the rules used for electing committee chairs, he was a shoe-in. After some last-minute behind-the-scenes attempts to prevent him from taking the chairmanship, Paul was elected unanimously. His close friend and colleague to the south, Mrs. Rose-Marie Ur, was similarly selected as government vice chair. The two promised to be a formidable team, a powerful voice for agriculture in south-western Ontario and across the country.

Accepting the job, Paul stated: "I am especially pleased to have been named chair, given the tremendous role that agriculture plays in Huron-Bruce. We are one of the most substantial agricultural producing regions in Canada, and as a farmer myself, I am eager to get started on the tasks ahead. Agriculture is an industry facing huge challenges, and I strongly believe that the Committee can play a useful role in outfitting our producers to successfully meet those challenges head on."[1] It is fair to say that Paul had no idea how "challenging" the years ahead actually would be.

---

1. Paul Steckle, MP, in a news release to Huron-Bruce media (Steckle to Chair Standing Committee on Agriculture and Agri-Food), February 4, 2003.

According to an old saying, "There is always a crisis in agriculture." This is true, not because farmers are doing anything wrong, but because the industry is so large and so diverse that the odds suggest there always will be a problem somewhere. Accordingly, the Commons Agriculture Committee never runs out of issues to explore or debate. In 2003, when Paul first assumed the Committee chairmanship, the matter placed on the table was bovine tuberculosis in the immediate vicinity of Riding Mountain National Park, which is located in Manitoba. In fact, that was the title of the Committee's first report that Paul presented to the House of Commons on April 10, 2003. The debate was fierce and the report profound, but it all fell by the wayside when the World Reference Laboratory confirmed on May 20, 2003, that an Alberta cow had tested positive for bovine spongiform encephalopathy. This disease, also know as BSE or "mad cow," was to dominate the next several years of the Canadian political agenda. At the time, most Canadians could not even pronounce bovine spongiform encephalopathy, but in the years that followed, BSE and the economic devastation that it caused were commonly understood on the streets of rural Canada.

Within hours of the formal announcement, the United States, Europe, and most of Canada's international trading partners slammed shut their borders to Canadian beef. Television stations such as CNN, CTV, CBC, and BBC, as well as most other major media outlets, reported that BSE was rampant in Canada. Dire images of sickly, staggering cattle and terminally ill humans who consumed contaminated meat began to dominate the media coverage. Of course, these pictures had been captured in the United Kingdom some years earlier, when thousands of cases of BSE surfaced in the domestic herd, including instances when the meat was consumed in the human food chain. No one cared that Canada's situation was nothing like the one in the UK, and as a result, fear, lack of concrete knowledge, and misinformation overwhelmed common sense and science. In its wake, farmers lost their life savings, entire rural communities teetered on the brink of insolvency, and governments scrambled to counteract the damage caused by the crisis.

The Standing Committee of Agriculture and Agri-Food swung into action. Just seven days after the news of the outbreak became public, Paul sat at the head of the table, during a special emergency session of the Standing Committee, in the Centre Block of Canada's gothic Parliamentary structure. Although Parliament was in recess for the summer, Paul and his co-chairs wanted to move immediately to see what was being done and what more could be done to help mitigate the anticipated fallout from the broadcasts. To quote the Committee's report:

> The occurrence on 20 May 2003 of a single case of bovine spongiform encephalopathy (BSE) in Alberta set off a chain reaction, the consequences of which were then unknown. It quickly became apparent, however, that it would have political, economic, trade, and social repercussions on the agriculture and agri-food sector in Canada—in the Western provinces, especially—for many months to come. The Standing Committee took immediate action and held its first special information session on 27 May with officials from the Canadian Food Inspection Agency (CFIA) and Agriculture and Agri-Food Canada (AAFC). Standing Committee members subsequently participated in various telephone conferences and, although Parliament had adjourned for the summer, they decided to assemble in Ottawa in order to meet with stakeholders in the various sectors of the cattle industry. These special meetings made it possible to follow the CFIA investigation and to discuss with government officials and stakeholders the measures taken by the government regarding compensation and diplomatic relations with Canada's trading partners, in the context of what may now be called the "mad cow crisis."[2]

That report, titled "The Investigation and the Government Response Following the Discovery of a Single Case of Bovine Spongiform Encephalopathy," was to be the first in a string of reports presented by the Standing

---

2. Introduction, the Investigation and the Government Response Following the Discovery of a Singles Case of Bovine Spongiform Encephalopathy (Report of the Standing Committee on Agriculture and Agri-Food), November 2003.

Committee of the day. Aside from dissecting the government's response to the crisis, the report called for seven specific actions:

1. The Standing Committee recommends that measures to ensure that specified risk materials are not included in animal feed be implemented, enforced, and audited for compliance.

2. The Standing Committee recommends that the federal government work, in cooperation with the CFIA, the industry, and provinces, to enhance the existing Canadian Cattle Identification Program by establishing a comprehensive and cost-effective national traceability system, as rapidly as possible.

3. The Standing Committee recommends the establishment of an industry/government task force that would focus specifically on the trade issues involved in the full restoration of export markets for livestock and its related meat products.

4. The Standing Committee recommends that the livestock industry and Parliament be kept informed on a regular basis of diplomatic efforts and trade missions conducted to improve Canada's livestock trade situation.

5. In order to ensure that the increased costs resulting from changes made to inspection, rendering practices, and traceability systems are not borne solely by livestock producers, the Standing Committee recommends that the Minister of Agriculture and Agri-Food increase the budget of the Canadian Food Inspection Agency. Furthermore, the Committee recommends that the Minister name an auditor to ensure that any additional costs be kept to a minimum and shared equitably among all stakeholders in the livestock sector.

6. The Standing Committee recommends a compensation plan for a culling program, which would include dairy cull cows, that should be conducted according to an attrition rate that would allow the industry to better balance supply and demand. Furthermore, since such a program will require the development of meat products with greater value added, the Committee recommends that the government support the industry through a special assistance fund for the development of new market opportunities.

7. The Standing Committee recommends that the Competition Bureau conduct an investigation into the pricing of beef at the processing and retail levels. To this end, the committee chair and five other members will send an official written request to the Bureau.

These seven simple recommendations—in particular, recommendation number seven—set into motion an unanticipated series of increasingly hostile events that eventually led to a confrontation between Paul Steckle and the five primary meat packing companies in Canada.

As phase two in the committee's review process, Paul Steckle rose in the House of Commons in April 2004 to table the second report of the Standing Committee. The document, titled "Canadian Livestock and Beef Pricing in the Aftermath of the BSE crisis," contained five recommendations. They were:

1. That the Minister of Industry instruct the Commissioner of Competition, under section 10 of the Competition Act, to conduct immediately an inquiry into the pricing of slaughter cattle and beef at the wholesale level.

2. That the Competition Bureau monitor the wholesale and retail pricing of beef, as well as the fed and feeder cattle prices, and that the Commissioner of Competition report periodically, or at the call of the chair, to the House of Commons Standing Committee on Agriculture and Agri-Food.

3. That the Government of Canada engage an independent body to conduct a comprehensive study of the competitive aspects of the cattle and beef products industry in Canada.

4. That the Government of Canada and its agencies involved in the agri-food sector work with livestock producers and processors to find new business opportunities in the livestock processing sector, with a particular emphasis on increasing livestock slaughter and value-added products processing capacity.

5. That the Governments of Canada and the United States immediately implement the World Organisation for Animal Health Code and repeal both countries' import embargoes, while continuing to

negotiate other modalities of an implementation plan that would improve the free flow of livestock and meat.

This represented the next salvo in the saga that was developing between Paul Steckle and the five meat packing companies in question. In the chair's foreword of that report, Paul connected the dots by noting:

> The House of Commons Standing Committee on Agriculture and Agri-Food conducted a study of "the pricing of beef at the slaughter, wholesale, and retail levels in the context of the BSE crisis in Canada." This study follows up on the Committee's report, [titled] "The Investigation and the Government Response Following the Discovery of a Single Case of Bovine Spongiform Encephalopathy," tabled in the House of Commons in November 2003. In that report, the Committee observed stable or slightly decreasing wholesale and retail prices for beef products in the face of sharply declining cattle prices. The Committee found this rather unresponsive pricing pattern disconcerting and therefore recommended that the Competition Bureau conduct an investigation into the pricing of beef at the processing and retail levels—a recommendation that was supported by an official written request to the Commissioner of Competition. In his letter of response on 3 December 2003, the Acting Commissioner of Competition stated that the Committee's report and hearings of 11 August 2003 did not "disclose any specific indication of an offence under the Competition Act had occurred"—a requirement under section 9(2) of the Act. Consequently, the Competition Bureau was not in a position to initiate an inquiry into the pricing of beef. Since that time, more data has been made available, which suggests that the situation has grown worse. In the aftermath of the BSE crisis, many industry experts and the public at large have observed cattle prices plummeting well below economically viable levels for many cattlemen. At the same time, the wholesale and retail prices of beef products have either risen or fallen by a much smaller proportion than cattle prices. The growing spread between farm-gate and retail prices has led many industry observers to express concern over the recent consolidation and rationalization within the packer and processing segment of the industry, which may have resulted in too much concentration of ownership. In the interest of pursuing these concerns, the Committee has continued its study of all potential explanations, including both competitive and anticompeti-

tive conduct, for the most recent increase in wholesale-to-farm-gate and retail-to-wholesale price spreads. Should any anticompetitive conduct on the part of vertically integrated operators be found, including any conspiracy to lower the prices of cattle in the bidding for supply, the adoption of predatory procurement policies (i.e., using their feedlot activities to cross-subsidize slaughterhouse activities with predatory intent), or the adoption of a policy to refuse to deal with any livestock producer or his agent, the Committee will recommend corrective measures to government. Indeed, the Committee will provide, in addition to this report, a letter and attachments of complaints and allegations made by industry stakeholders to the Minister of Agriculture and Agri-Food, the Minister of Industry and the Commissioner of Competition.

In simple terms, the auction price of cattle had plummeted while the price of beef, paid at the grocery store by consumers, had not. More importantly, the committee believed that there was reason to suspect that at least one of these packing houses was profiting from the crisis via intimidation and other anti-competitive acts. These were very serious allegations, and, for obvious reasons, the corporations in question denied the charges with vigour. The committee responded by seeking to hold meetings to explore the notion that these packing houses had committed anti-competitive acts, while at the same time siphoning off government assistance money that was intended to provide financial relief to beleaguered beef farmers. The committee demanded access to the private and confidential proprietary information contained within the internal financial statements of the packing houses. The packers endeavoured to decline or ignore the request, viewing the committee and its request as irrelevant. With that, the stage was set—and the fight was on.

In the days and weeks that followed, tension between the groups escalated to unprecedented proportions. At one particular nationally televised committee meeting, armed security personnel were in attendance. Posted both in plain sight at the doors and undercover in the audience, these officers were to ensure that the civility of a House of Commons hearing was maintained. While they were present in direct response to a death threat that had been directed at Paul Steckle, their job, in a more general sense, was to provide a sense of calm for all those involved. A whispered, allegedly private, and off-the-cuff remark had caught the attention of House of Commons Security and the RCMP: "If Steckle isn't careful they may find him in a Dumpster." They were not taking any chances. The threat of subpoenas had been employed by the committee to bring the formal encounter to fruition, and the television cameras were rolling.

In the end, the real tension breaker was an election. On the eve of the dissolution of the Thirty-seventh Parliament of Canada, an order was unanimously approved that read:

> That the House of Commons find Cargill Foods, Lakeside Packers, and Levinoff Meats Limited in contempt and order them to provide, before Monday, 10 May, 2004, at noon (EDT), to the Clerk of the Standing Committee on Agriculture and Agri-Food, who will maintain the following documents in accordance to the 21 April 2004, motion (a) a copy of the financial statements detailing the added marginal costs attributable to the new BSE safety regulations along with their profit margins on a monthly basis for calendar year 2003; and (b) documents explaining why the prices they paid for fed steers, heifers, cows and bulls declined by approximately 50 per cent in the three weeks following the announcement of the federal-provincial BSE Recovery Program on 18 June 2003.

The Conservative Official Opposition blocked the acceptance of a subsequent order which read:

> That the House of Commons find that Cargill Foods and Lakeside Packers remain in contempt of the House of Commons. If after a further delay to produce documents by May 20, 2004, at 3:00 PM (EDT), the said production of documents is not complied with, each of these companies shall pay a fine of $250,000 for each day, or part of a day, commencing at 12:01 AM (EDT), May 21, 2004, until they comply with the request stated in the Committee's letter of May 11, 2004. Such fines shall be payable to the Receiver General of Canada, and they shall be considered a debt owing to Her Majesty in Right of Canada and may be enforced through any avenue of recourse available to Her Majesty in Right of Canada.

Paul was furious; he truly believed that at least one (if not more) of the packers had been involved in a scheme to unfairly dominate the marketplace on the backs of innocent beef farmers. The truth seemed clear, even if from a legal and factual perspective it was anything but clear; that is, there was no "smoking gun." Now, with the Conservatives seemingly "in bed" with the alleged culprits, there was little more that Paul could do. He had been the subject of personal death threats; he had expended countless hours and thousands of dollars in committee resources; and now, to make matters worse, the Conservatives maintained in the election campaign that they did not prevent the acceptance of the said contempt of Parliament monetary punishment. In a world where perception quickly morphs into reality, all was to be lost in the confusing haze of the canvas. Frustration did not even begin to cover what Paul was feeling.

On a personal level, the campaign returned Paul to office with a healthy victory. His ten-thousand-vote margin was at least some solace. The Liberal Party was returned to government, but the Committee would have to restart the entire process again. New committee members, the procedural requirement for reconstitution of the body, and the loss of trust among the parliamentarians hindered the process. The precedent-setting contempt of Parliament declaration, the first of its kind in hundreds of years, was gone, but the message remained. This parliamentary committee and its tenacious chair were not going to go away easily. Co-operation was the only option.

In the months that followed, co-operation came more readily. Roles, power, and responsibilities were more clearly defined. In the end, the committee was never able to prove that illegal or immoral activities had transpired, but the spotlight was now warmed up, and businesses in all sectors of the Canadian economy were on notice. Government programming was re-evaluated, with the goal of preventing such perceptions of impropriety, real or otherwise, from occurring in the future. While Paul Steckle had not managed to hang the noose around anyone's neck, he had clearly set the standard by which committees would operate in the future. They were not toothless debating clubs; they could make a difference. The Agriculture Committee had taken its place as a leader and trend-setter among similar legislative bodies. Never again would committee clerks, researchers, and staff secretly single out the Agriculture Committee as bland, boring, or sleepy. It was high-profile, dynamic, and nothing if not interesting—a designation that could only serve the committee well in its future pursuit of answers to the questions that farmers ask.

Chapter 14

Married to Tradition

As you know, my position on this matter is clear and public. In fact, on June 8, 1999, I voted to support a motion in the House of Commons that stated: "That, in the opinion of this House, it is necessary, in light of public debate around recent court decisions, to state that marriage is and should remain the union of one man and one woman to the exclusion of all others, and that Parliament will take all steps within the jurisdiction of the Parliament of Canada to preserve this definition of marriage in Canada" (Source: Hansard (Tuesday, June 8, 1999) Page 15960). At the time I was very pleased to see that Cabinet (you included) and most of Caucus supported this motion. In fact, it should be noted that the justice minister of the day (Anne McLellan) supported the motion and was subsequently quoted in the *Montreal Gazette* (June 9, 1999) as saying, "A marriage is a union between one man and one woman ... We on this side of the House agree that the institution of marriage is a central and important institution in the lives of many Canadians. Indeed, worldwide, it plays an important part in all society, second only to the fundamental importance of family." Needless to say, I am truly saddened by the complete policy reversal that is now taking place.

—Paul Steckle, MP
In a letter to Paul Martin, MP, for LaSalle-Émard
September 2004

"Until death do you part" is most commonly heard during a traditional Christian wedding ceremony, but it seems to me that the idiom would be more apropos if applied to how the institution of marriage and the public career of Paul Steckle are intertwined. In the beginning, Paul was nudged to Liberalism as a direct result of what he would later call "the marriage issue." In actual fact, the issue of same-sex marriage and homosexual rights in general dominated Paul's career in federal politics.

Paul was first elected to the Thirty-fifth Parliament of Canada, which ran between January 17, 1994, and April 27, 1997. He was subsequently re-elected to the Thirty-sixth (September 22, 1997–October 22, 2000); the Thirty-seventh (January 29, 2001–May 23, 2004); the Thirty-eighth (October 4, 2004–November 29, 2005); and the Thirty-ninth (April 3, 2006–present) Parliaments. In each of those sessions, the issue of homosexual rights was fiercely debated, and new laws were enacted as a result.

In the Thirty-fifth Parliament of Canada (First Session), Bill C-41, an Act to Amend the Criminal Code (Hate Crimes), was introduced and passed. This legislation made homosexuals a legally recognized "identifiable group," against whom a hate crime could be perpetrated. It provided for increased penalties for those who committed crimes against the gay community. In the Second Session of that same Parliament, Bill C-33, an Act to Amend the Canadian Human Rights Act, was enacted. This legislation added sexual orientation to the list of prohibited grounds of discrimination under the Canadian Human Rights Act. In the Thirty-sixth Parliament of Canada (First Session), Paul was a participant in what was to be the first round of the looming same-sex marriage debate. To that end, on June 8, 1999, the House of Commons proclaimed: "That, in the opinion of this House, it is necessary, in light of public debate around recent court decisions, to state that marriage is and should remain the union of one man and one woman to the exclusion of all others, and that Parliament will take all steps within the jurisdiction of the Parliament of Canada to preserve this definition of marriage in Canada."

The said motion was contentious for some, but it passed by a vote of 216 to 55. The very next day, the Minister of Justice added to the debate by stating, "A marriage is a union between one man and one woman ... We on this side (of the Commons) agree that the institution of marriage is a central and important institution in the lives of many Canadians. Indeed, worldwide, it plays an important part in all society, second only to the fundamental importance of family."[1] While the entire matter appeared to have passed from the political radar screen, only a few months later, during the Second Session of the Thirty-sixth Parliament, Bill C-23 was introduced. Bill C-23, an Act to Modernize the Statutes of Canada in Relation to Benefits and Obligations, amended over 60 federal statutes in a manner that permitted same-sex partners who were engaged in a "conjugal" relationship to receive the same societal benefits provided to opposite-sex couples.

Mirroring the sentiments of literally hundreds of letters from residents of Huron-Bruce, Paul was not pleased with the idea of premising marital tax benefits on "conjugality." After all, was it not Pierre Trudeau who suggested that "the state has no place in the bedrooms of the nation"? Not more than two generations after those words were first spoken, we, as a society, were again, at the very least, peering through the keyhole into the bedrooms of the nation. As a compromise, Paul Steckle suggested that all those concerned heed Mr. Trudeau's words and extend certain societal benefits to all dependency relationships, rather than simply to those engaged in a permanent or long-term physical association. With that in mind, on February 21, 2000, Paul spoke in the House of Commons:

> Each and every day we pass laws and regulations that are supposed to improve the quality of life for all Canadians. In fact, earlier today, we gave Bill C-23 its second reading. It's no secret that this bill, which amends over 60 pieces of legislation to extend spousal benefits to same-sex couples, is highly controversial. It is also no secret that I am not supportive of this legislation. I would like to take this opportunity to again reiterate that I am not supporting this legislation due to the fact that it recognizes financial dependency only in cases where there is conjugality. Yes, Mr. Speaker, as silly as it seems, apparently Mr. Trudeau was wrong, and the state does indeed belong in the bedrooms

---

1. Hon. Anne McLellan, PC, MP, Minister of Justice, quoted by Tim Naumetz, Same-sex union isn't marriage: McLellan (*The Montreal Gazette*, June 9, 1999), A1.

of the nation! As you know, Mr. Speaker, I represent the best riding in all of Canada. Moreover, Huron-Bruce is primarily rural in nature. This fact often creates a situation where extended families are financially required to band together so as to maintain functionality. I can name numerous dependency relationships, such as those involving two siblings or even a child and an elderly parent. I would ask you, Mr. Speaker, why are these relationships less deserving of benefits or less financially or emotionally dependent on one another than a same-sex couple engaged in a relationship based upon conjugality? The short answer is that they are not less deserving. As we all know, the Supreme Court of Canada has determined, in accordance with the Charter of Rights and Freedoms, that society can not discriminate. With this in mind, I would respectfully suggest that if we fail to recognize all dependency relationships, we are simply exchanging one form of discrimination for another ... I am promoting an inclusionist policy. Let's heed Mr. Trudeau's famous words and draw the shades. If we are going to extend benefits, then let us extend benefits to all of those engaged in a verifiable relationship based upon dependency[2].

Paul's proposal was disregarded by government, and the notions contained within Bill C-23 were complemented and strengthened when, on June 12, 2003, the House Justice Committee of the Thirty-seventh Parliament voted nine to eight in favour of changing the traditional definition of marriage. In response, Paul was quoted in the riding media: "This is totally unacceptable. I cannot believe that some members of the committee would seek to dismantle an institution such as marriage. I intend to work to see that the government does not accept this committee decision and that, indeed, we live up to our previous commitment to preserve traditional heterosexual marriage. I believe that Parliament's will supersedes that of any committee."[3] With those few simple words, the wick was lit on what was to become the most pronounced change in Canadian social policy since the beginning of WWI.

---

2. Paul Steckle, MP, in a presentation to the House of Commons, February 21, 2000.
3. Paul Steckle, MP, in a press release issued to (and subsequently printed in) Huron-Bruce media sources (Steckle Denounces the Decision of the Justice Committee), June 12, 2003.

It should be noted that while the Liberal Party of Canada seemed to be leading the charge for an enhanced set of homosexual rights, the position was far from unanimous. As just one example of the divisions that existed within the caucus, on April 11, 2000, subsequent to the resumption of the third reading debate on Bill C-23, a gay rights motion, proposed by the minister of justice passed by a count of 176 votes to 72. Of that number, 17 Liberals were amongst those who voted to defeat the measure.

At that point, the entire issue seemed to temporarily fade into the background ... or so it seemed at the time—that is, until July 12, 2002, when the Ontario Divisional Court ruled by a two to one vote that excluding same-sex couples the institution of marriage was discriminatory and thus unconstitutional in Canada. The result was that unless appealed, the government would have two years to alter all existing laws so as to reflect and recognize the decision.

This set into motion a tremendous series of events that culminated in a chaotic election campaign that perpetuated a likewise environment during the opening days of the Thirty-eighth Parliament (following the election of June 28, 2004). Again, the same-sex marriage debate not only appeared but dominated the national political stage. While the Conservative Party of Ontario openly supported the concept, the federal Liberals, the NDP at all levels, and Bloc in Ottawa were largely seen as the driving forces behind the movement. Paul remained steadfast with respect to his on-the-record support that "a marriage is a union between one man and one woman," but he was prepared to continue to support the notion of alternate dependency relationships. Many constituents in Huron-Bruce opposed such a notion, but Paul viewed it as a potential way to appease both sides of the issue. Of course, there were those on the pro-same-sex marriage side of the debate that wanted no part of Paul's dependency relationship proposal.

In an April 2005 letter to one of his own constituents, Paul responded to concerns about the plan:

> I am writing in response to your facsimile, received by this office on March 29, 2005, in which you ask for clarification on my voting intentions with respect to same-sex marriage. Specifically, you express your personal concerns and reservations with the idea of an alternate,

same-sex civil union. Let me begin by again saying that I will not vote to alter the traditional definition of marriage. As I have underscored in several pieces of correspondence to you over the past several years, my position is clear on this matter. I believe that marriage is a holy union, ordained by God, which should be maintained for one man and one woman, exclusively. I have spoken publicly and voted according to this ideal on several occasions in the past, and I can imagine no circumstance or event that would alter this practice in the future. Again, for the purposes of absolute clarity, I do not support same-sex marriage, and I will cast my vote in the House of Commons accordingly ... In my opinion, retention of the traditional definition of marriage is not about discrimination against same-sex partners. It is about retaining a core building block of human society. Marriage is a biblical institution that is different from any other. With this in mind, as I have stated in the past, I would be prepared to explore the idea of an alternate civil union, as this would recognize the dependency relationship without altering an ancient institution that is rooted in almost universal religious philosophy. I would not base this concept on conjugality but rather on financial dependency. Again, I am suggesting that such a "union" would not be based upon conjugality and therefore, sexual orientation would be irrelevant. Lastly, *if absolutely necessary to protect the sanctity of marriage*, I would also be prepared to accept that solemnization should be the exclusive responsibility of the churches, contrary to the current practice of state solemnization. I offer the above as alternatives if it is determined that traditional marriage cannot exist exclusively within the Canadian legal system. While I do not accept that this is the case, I am not a Supreme Court justice and as such, I do not have the legal authority to make that determination. My job as a legislator is to function within the bounds of my Constitutional role, and I am endeavouring to do just that. My goal is to protect marriage, and I am not just working in the present-day to accomplish this. I must also proactively strive to prepare for challenges that have not yet developed.[4]

That is truthfully the crux of the entire matter. Paul didn't believe that dependency relationship recognition was the best option, but he believed

---

4. Paul Steckle, MP, in a letter to a constituent (the constituent's name has been omitted from this publication for privacy reasons), received April 7, 2005.

that it was a better option than full recognition of same-sex marriage. Eventually, all talk of dependency recognition fell by the wayside, and the debate centred exclusively on the issue of same-sex marriage as an equitable and comparable institution to traditional opposite-sex marriage in the eyes of the law.

Paul lobbied and was lobbied by nearly every conceivable group. Other MPs, senators, partisan leadership, special-interest groups and private citizens all engaged in the process. The offices in Goderich and Ottawa received more than twelve thousand calls, letters, e-mails, faxes and visits on the subject. Some of the incoming correspondence was quite complex and provocative, while still other items, such as an unsigned Post-it note stuck to the door of the Goderich constituency office one morning, were crudely written and namelessly delivered. That specific note read, simply, "Don't be a faggot." For the most part, the correspondence was not hate-filled; it expressed a genuine concern that same-sex marriage posed a threat to traditional marriage from a biblical perspective.

In an attempt to gauge constituent thoughts more fully, Paul sent a circular to every household in Huron-Bruce in August 2003. The questionnaire asked three simple yet direct questions about same-sex marriage:

1. Should same-sex marriage be legalized?

2. Should governments recognize a same-sex civil union?

3. If a parliamentary free vote rejects same-sex marriage, should the Notwithstanding Clause be used to maintain the current legal definition of marriage?

The answers were equally clear. In response to the first question, of those who responded, the answer was 16 per cent in favour and 83 per cent against. The second resulted in a 36 per cent in favour; 59 per cent against. And the third questions garnered 62 per cent in favour; 26 per cent against.

In the end, the results of the survey seemed to parallel the ratios that the office staff had been tracking in the inward-bound communications received from constituents. It would seem that, scientific or not,

Huron-Bruce was not prepared to readily accept same-sex marriage, and they expected their federal representative to carry their voice to the table.

In this instance, Paul Steckle was one of the 83 per cent who opposed same-sex marriage. While public media releases from the office were word-smithed to fit the situation, the fact is that Paul opposed same-sex marriage outright. In 2004, when the Minister of Justice and Attorney General of Canada served notice that he intended to introduce legislation that would redefine traditional marriage in a manner that would legalize same-sex unions, the simmering battle was brought to a head. In response, on January 28, 2005, Paul articulated his views in a speech to the South-Huron Ministerial Directive, which includes a multi-denominational audience of clergy. He said:

> I want to make you aware of the specific intricacies, history, misconceptions, rhetoric and truths that are now making their way into the homes and minds of your parishioners via coffee shop talk and the national media. I believe that it is important that you understand that I am not seeking to "spin" my message to agree with any one partisan position but rather, I am offering a frank and honest assessment of the issue of same-sex marriage as I see it … Complacency and silence breed a situation whereby political correctness can reign supreme. Active involvement and participation by a well-informed, level-headed, and determined population can serve to remind our leaders that they are to be the voice of the people and not the voice to the people.[5]

Paul spoke on a range of issues relating to the history of the entire matter, but in the four points that he specifically addressed during his discussion with the pastors (recent legislative chronology, his personal thoughts, the Supreme Court ruling, and the Charter), his personal thoughts seemed to garner the most attention. I am certain that he did not know how true his words were, even though he prefaced his remarks by saying, "In the past week I have garnered much attention in the national media and in

---

5. Paul Steckle, MP, in a speech to the South Huron Ministerial Directive. January 28, 2005.

doing so, I have opened myself up to the name-calling and criticism that so often follows when one opts to take a stand on any issue of conscious."

Within moments of the conclusion of Paul's remarks, Reverend Charlie Love, a United Church Minister in Bayfield, spoke to the media and suggested that Paul was a racist. Reverend Love was offended when Paul recounted the biblical story of Isaac and Ishmael. Reverend Love was quoted in Eric Collins' *Lakeshore Advance* story as saying, "While making an argument against polygamy, Steckle recalled the Abraham story and the birth of Ishmael as an example of polygamy and then said something to the effect of 'and out of Ishmael a whole nation was born and look where that got us.'" While it makes for a very good story, I might point out that Reverend Love used the words "and then said something to the effect of …" In short, he could not recall Paul's exact words, yet he was prepared to deride Paul in the local media. Indeed, this example shows how easy it is to cast aspersions rather than seek out truth and clarification—a practice that is regrettably commonplace when politics collides with entrenched or deeply held beliefs. Paul simply responded by saying, "I have never intended to, nor do I intend to from here on in, to ever slander a group of people, in particular when they are not there to speak for themselves." He went on to say of Reverend Love, "There is an entitlement we have, and all of us do treasure that freedom in this country, where everyone has a right to their thoughts … [This includes] the gentleman who has taken question to my comments."[6]

The issue was far from over. In a letter to the editor, printed in local papers the very next week, Paul Ciufo, a Grand Bend resident, called Paul's comments reprehensible. He compared Paul's remarks to those found in "Nazi Germany, the former Yugoslavia, Rwanda and many other societies." With this as justification, Mr. Ciufo demanded that Paul "take steps to atone, or resign."[7] While I would not criticise anyone for his beliefs, I was somewhat surprised at the viciousness of Mr. Ciufo's

6. Eric Collins, Huron-Bruce MP reaffirms stance on same-sex marriage in Canada (*The Lakeshore Advance*), February 2, 2005.
7. Paul Ciufo, in a letter to the editor of *The Lakeshore Advance*, February 9, 2005.

remarks, especially since he was not present when Paul spoke to the South-Huron Ministerial Directive, nor did any media article, to my knowledge, print the actual text of Paul's remarks that day. Anger and outrage, it seems, are easy to come by; maintaining calm while searching for the truth is obviously much harder. In the end, Mr. Ciufo did call Paul to privately express his regrets for what he said in the media.

For the sake of posterity, here is what Paul actually said that day, in part, to the South-Huron Ministerial Directive. I believe that it is worth mentioning that on March 21, 2005, Paul gave a similar dissertation in the House of Commons. The complete text of that speech is available on the parliamentary intranet.

> Plainly put, I strongly believe that the institution of "marriage" should remain confined to opposite-sex couples. I strongly support the stand that federal lawyers took in the Ontario court when they said that marriage embodies the complementary of the two human sexes—it is not simply a shopping list of functional attributes, but a unique, opposite-sex bond that is common across different times, cultures, and religions, as a virtually universal norm. Marriage is a relationship that is as old as time itself. It existed prior to our laws and is a core building block of modern society that must be preserved. I would also like to take a moment to address my thoughts as they pertain to homosexuals and homosexuality, in general.
>
> 1. I believe that we have all been placed on this earth by God, a supreme being from which all life springs forth.
>
> 2. I do not feel hate towards homosexuals; however, I do believe that homosexuality is a sin. My Bible reads "Judge not, lest ye will be judged." In modern language, condemn the act but never the person. In the end, we will all face our ultimate judgment, and I do not have the capacity to prejudge with certainty how any person will fare when adjudicated by the Almighty.
>
> 3. While I believe that all people, regardless of their sexual orientation, have the capacity to feel love in equal measure, I do not accept that a homosexual relationship is the same as a heterosexual one. I believe that marriage is a unique state of being; a relation-

ship [that] is ordained by God for purposes that go beyond simple procreation and financial security.

4. Marriage is an institution that predates our legal system. I believe that it was a divine creation that man does not have the authority or mandate to alter to complement issues of the day.

All in all, retention of the traditional definition of marriage is not about discrimination against same-sex partners. It is about retaining a core building block of human society. Marriage is a biblical institution that is different [from] any other. With this in mind, I would be prepared to explore the idea of an alternate civil union, as this would recognize the dependency relationship without altering an ancient institution that is rooted in almost universal religious philosophy. If absolutely necessary to protect the sanctity of marriage, I would also be prepared to accept that solemnization should be the exclusive responsibility of the churches, contrary to the current practice of state solemnization[8].

In the portions of his speech that pertained to the Supreme Court ruling on the subject, Paul stated:

The Supreme Court of Canada did not rule on whether or not the traditional definition of marriage is unconstitutional, because by not appealing the lower court decisions on the matter, the government had already indicated that it intended to make same-sex marriage legal ... At a minimum ... I believe that in the absence of clarification from either the courts or the Department of Justice, we, as legislators and as citizens, must step to the plate and make certain that no stone is left unturned ... Until these points are given further clarity or there is an adequate explanation as to why the concerns outlined above are without merit, it would be impossible for me to support the proposed legislation as I now understand it ... Personally, I am not prepared to vote in favour of same-sex marriage for the reasons I have set upon the table today.[9]

---

8. Paul Steckle, MP, in a presentation in the House of Commons, March 21, 2005. This text was also contained in the speech given by Paul Steckle, MP, to the South Huron Ministerial Directive on January 28, 2005.
9. Paul Steckle, MP, in a presentation in the House of Commons on March 21, 2005.

While the text does not include any of his ad-lib commentary, it is worth mentioning that subsequent to the furor erupting in the papers, Paul received several notes of encouragement from clergy who were, in fact, in the audience that day. While they are too numerous to print in their entirety, here is the text of one such note:

> Hi, Paul. Just wanted to encourage you this week, especially in light of the debate surrounding the potential reopening of the marriage debate. Please be sure of my prayers for you this week. May you have the courage to stand for righteousness and the good of children and the home. Thanks for the leadership you have demonstrated and the strength of character you model.[10]

---

10. An e-mail, from a Huron County clergyman (the name has been omitted for privacy reasons), to Paul Steckle, MP, received by Paul Steckle, MP, on March 23, 2005.

Chapter 15

The Leader Is Good

Paul [Steckle]'s a nice guy, even if I don't like his party. He is an honourable man who believes in representing his constituents. I'll have to have a chat with him and tell him to come home to the Canadian Alliance, because he won't get elected where he is next time.

—Stockwell Day, MP
Leader of the Canadian Alliance
At a pre-election visit to Holmesville, Ontario
June 17, 2000

Paul Steckle's name has appeared on the list of accredited delegates for every national Liberal Leadership Convention since 1968. His proclivity for supporting winners, while not perfect, is certainly pronounced and impressive. Over the years, Paul has supported Paul Hellyer, Jean Chrétien, Paul Martin, and Stéphane Dion in their respective bids to become the leader of the most successful political party in the Western Hemisphere. Paul also has a history of expecting his leadership candidates to devise and implement an effective and timely exit strategy.

In 1990 Jean Chrétien was elected as the Liberal leader in an impressive first-ballot victory with 56.81 per cent (2652 votes) of the 4668 votes cast at the Calgary convention. Following that victory, Mr. Chrétien went on to lead the party to three consecutive majority government victories, starting in 1993; the first time that feat had been attained since Sir Wilfrid Laurier's third majority government in 1909 (Eleventh Parliament of Canada; January 20, 1909–July 29, 1911). Despite this nearly unprecedented electoral success, Paul Steckle was one of the first members of the elected Liberal caucus to announce his belief that Mr. Chrétien's time as the party leader should be over. Obviously, Paul's statements coincided with constituent feedback, but it could be argued that his political instincts, mixed with a no-nonsense, straight-to-the-point attitude, overruled any partisan loyalties that might have been due to the leader of the day. More specifically, given that Paul and Mr. Chrétien had butted heads over the years, it also is feasible that Paul simply abandoned the current leader in favour of another seemingly brighter and rising star.

That star was most certainly Paul Martin. The two Pauls had worked closely over the years, and in that time they developed a friendship. Paul Martin maintained a family cottage in Huron-Bruce and spent many summers as a teen in the area. He visited the area as Finance Minister and had worked with Paul on issues such as the Notional Input Tax Credit, and the two seemingly shared the same fiscal conservatism. All things considered, they seemed a natural fit.

Paul Steckle's support of Paul Martin was not something that began when Mr. Martin became prime minister. Paul Steckle had been a long-time supporter; in the years when Martin was the finance minister, Paul Steckle routinely had gone on the record as a "Martinite." In July 2002, Paul publicly came to Martin's defence by responding to a constituent's letter to the editor that had been printed in a local paper. Paul's response letter read:

> Firstly, the writer in the original letter claims that Paul Martin did nothing to bring order to the nation's finances. In his words, "Paul Martin was one very lucky finance minister." What he failed to mention was that prior to Mr. Martin, no Canadian minister of finance since 1969 had managed to balance the budget. Moreover, Mr. Martin also managed to balance multiple consecutive budgets, something that

had not been accomplished in Canada in half a century. Additionally, I should also mention that when Mr. Martin first became the minister of finance, the deficit stood at $42 billion. That amount of annual over-spending, when heaped upon our already massive nation debt, caused Canadian taxpayers to borrow nearly $50 billion per year in interest alone. Today, due largely to the direction provided by Mr. Martin, the Government of Canada is running regular budgetary surpluses. In fact, according to the last budget, that surplus is almost $18 billion. This money, along with surpluses from the previous three years, has reduced the principal of our unmatured national debt by $31 billion. While it is true that the debt continued to grow until 1996, most people will understand that you must first stop overspending prior to paying off your credit cards. It took Paul Martin only three years to stop that overspending, an accomplishment that eluded all of his predecessors since the 1960s. Looking at it from this perspective, I would suggest that we were very lucky to have Paul Martin as our finance minister. Secondly, with respect to the statement "Paul Martin has achieved sur-pluses by cutting back on transfer payments to the provinces for healthcare" … this lunacy barely warrants a response. The only thing more ridiculous than this rubbish would be to suggest that it was the Mulroney government that put us on the path to fiscal well-being (something that the writer did later in his correspondence). In 1993, when Martin first became minister of finance, the federal transfer pay-ments to the Province of Ontario totaled $10.3 billion. Today, the annual transfer payment to Ontario totals $14.5 billion, a $4.2 billion increase in Ontario alone. This amount constitutes 20 per cent of Ontario's total revenues ($1,108 per person). While I am no econo-mist, this seems positive to me.

That letter was not the first, nor was it the last public argument that Paul Steckle waded into with respect to Paul Martin. In the early days, the letters were in defence of Mr. Martin, but as time moved forward, the Pauls developed serious policy differences.

Like his predecessor, Paul Martin won the Liberal Party leadership on the first ballot. In fact, the November 14, 2003, Toronto-based conven-tion would be more aptly described as a coronation than a contest. On the first round of voting Paul Martin received 93.84 per cent (3242 votes) of the possible 3455 votes. His only competitor, Sheila Copps, received 6.11

per cent or 211 votes. While his numeric victory was decisive, Paul Martin had an uphill battle to wage if he was to successfully lead the party—there had been a long-time civil war within the Liberal Party. The fragmentation only grew worse in the years between 2003 and 2006. The Liberals were reduced to a minority government status following the 2004 election campaign and were swept out of office altogether following the disastrous campaign of 2005/2006. It was during this last campaign that Paul Steckle found himself most at odds with his old friend the Prime Minister.

During that campaign, the once-organized and -focused Liberal machine waned dramatically. Under pressure from scandal, facing character assassination at the hands of a politically motivated RCMP investigation, fighting the elements, and a scattered and misguided internal policy development process, the party failed to build upon its past successes. In the end, the electorate's desire for change swept the Paul Martin Liberals from power. While Paul Steckle narrowly held on to his seat, he was now a member of Her Majesty's Official Opposition. The election campaign had been bitter and had opened several rifts between Paul and "Team Martin." While he was much less vocal out of respect for Mr. Martin, Paul was no less angry with those responsible for the decline of the party. The deterioration had happened over the course of years, and in the wake of the January 23, 2006, defeat, most within the party understood that it would take time to restore the lustre.

Almost immediately, Paul Steckle and the rest of the Liberal caucus and party began the rebuilding and renewal efforts. Bill Graham, a Toronto-area MP and former cabinet minister, was selected to fill the post of interim leader. Each MP and senator began to focus on areas falling within his or her unique range of skills. For Paul Steckle, that meant rural affairs.

On April 24, 2006, Paul signed a letter to Mr. Graham. That letter, among other things, stressed the importance of the creation of a rural affairs critic. Paul further noted:

> As you know and have both privately and publicly acknowledged, the Liberal Party of Canada is today facing a serious challenge. In the most recent election the party was virtually shut out of rural Canada due largely to a policy platform that was, for the most part, urban focused. The National Liberal Caucus was

stripped of several quality rural representatives, as rural Canadians recognized that our party was adrift with respect to the unique issues facing Canadians residing outside of the major metropolitan areas of the country. Consequently, while we managed to electorally dominate the major cities, we were decimated in rural Canada. The resulting loss of seats has relegated the Liberal Party to Opposition status, something that from an electoral math perspective will not change unless we recapture those lost seats in rural Canada. With the above in mind, I am writing today to solicit your personal intervention in an effort to dispel the myth that the Liberal Party of Canada is an urban party. To do this, as a start, I am suggesting the following:

1. Rural Canada is more than simply agriculture. It is a complex weave of issues ranging from rural healthcare and rural mail delivery to economic development and infrastructure renewal. We currently have more than 40 critics, but while we recognize an agricultural critic, we have failed to assign a critic for rural affairs. We continually fail to recognize that even basic national issues are uniquely received in rural Canada. As an example, while all Canadians care about healthcare, rural Canadians face very specific and specialized challenges in this area. With an aging population this is perhaps one of the areas of greatest concern facing all rural Canadians. Our hospitals are suffering from a serious doctor shortage. That, coupled with an aging infrastructure, technological limitations, and various demographic and geographic challenges, has placed an increasing strain on rural healthcare systems and providers. Specialized problems require specialized solutions, and I believe that the National Liberal Caucus should immediately appoint a critic for rural affairs.

2. The Liberal Party of Canada must immediately appoint a qualified person to conduct a fulsome rural policy review and creation process. Rural policy should not be lumped in with general policy development. Rural policy is the key to our returning to government and, as such, must be given the attention that it deserves. Most notions and policies currently in place need to be cast out in favour of a complete rural and agricultural policy review. We need to get serious about rural Canada if we want them to get serious about the Liberal Party of Canada ...

> I offer these ... simple suggestions in an effort to provide construc-
> tive feedback as the party begins to rebuild, retool, and reinvent itself
> on many fronts. I would be pleased to discuss anything contained
> herein.[1]

Almost immediately, the office received a call from Andy Mitchell, Chief of Staff to the Interim Leader. A meeting was convened, and a short time later the rural affairs critic posting was established. Additionally, in keeping with the second of his recommendations, Paul also launched a comprehensive review of the party's rural policy platform in co-operation with the National Liberal Rural Caucus. After an extensive consultation process and considerable research, Paul presented a discussion paper to the rural caucus. The document, titled "Rural Canada: sharing the wealth beyond tomorrow," contained 33 recommendations and was adopted unanimously by the National Liberal Rural Caucus on June 6, 2006. The document was subsequently presented to the National Liberal Caucus on July 7, 2006. The counsel contained therein represented a massive reshaping of Liberal Party policy as it related to rural Canada and the agricultural sector in general.

These efforts continued into the December 2006 party leadership, where the delegates endorsed a number of the proposals and established them as official party policy. Items, such as the establishment of a rural affairs cabinet minister, no longer existed only in Paul Steckle's thoughts. Those ideas would now be implemented if and when the party formed government again. Paul Steckle and all those who contributed to the effort had left their mark.

On December 3, 2006, at Montreal's Palais des Cogrès, Stéphane Dion, the former Chrétien recruit and Martin cabinet minister, became the leader of the Liberal Party of Canada in a surprising and exhilarating upset. Although he was in third place with 17.8 per cent of the vote following the first ballot, Dion went on to win the contest with 54.7 per cent

---

1. Paul Steckle, MP, in a letter to Hon. Bill Graham, PC, MP, Interim Leader of the Official Opposition and Leader of the Liberal Party of Canada, April 24, 2006.

of the vote, edging out the front-runner, Michael Ignatieff, on the fourth ballot. Dion, the underdog candidate, received an astounding 2521 votes, which propelled him into the new job. The intellectually driven Member of Parliament for Saint-Laurent Cartierville (Montreal) was now the leader of the party—a party in transition. Paul Steckle, who was one of only a handful of caucus members who had supported Dion from the beginning, was thrilled. He remarked:

> Since he was first elected as a federal MP a decade ago, I have worked with Stéphane as both a colleague and as a personal friend. Aside from his obvious sincerity, integrity, and intelligence, I have found Stéphane to be a committed member of the House of Commons, with a deep devotion to the philosophies and values of Canada and the Liberal Party. His reputation is beyond reproach, and his many accomplishments speak to the intensity of his personal abilities. It is for these reasons and more that I am proud to offer my support to Stéphane Dion as he seeks the leadership of the Liberal Party of Canada … In the weeks and months ahead, I will be working with the Dion leadership team to help raise the overall calibre of debate in the leadership process. I will push for greater attention to rural affairs, especially on those areas addressed by the thirty-three recommendations contained within the recently released National Liberal Rural Caucus Report. I am proud that Stéphane is fully committed to finding a resolution to the many complex issues facing rural Canada.[2]

The year 2007 marked the beginning of Paul Steckle's 14th calendar year as the MP for Huron-Bruce. During his time, there have been four party leaders and five general elections. His role has advanced from rookie recruit to senior advisor, policy developer, and mentor. On December 4, 2006, the day after the most recent leadership convention, Paul Steckle awoke, had breakfast and a coffee, and then sat at his desk in his Stanley Township home. He now had a new role, with new expectations and new

---

2. Paul Steckle, MP, in a news release, issued subsequent to the Liberal Party of Canada's 2006 Summer Caucus meeting in Vancouver, BC, August 23, 2006.

challenges. He pondered that for a moment, and then he picked up the phone and made the first step on that journey.

Chapter 16

A Picture Is Worth a Thousand Words

I had to think—is this really a news issue?
It must be a slow news day.

—Paul Steckle, MP
Clinton News Record
December 22, 2004

For most of us, the lead-up to the Christmas season is a tremendously hectic time, at best. We run furiously from store to store, searching for that perfect gift; we attend our office or community Christmas parties and school concerts; we prepare copious amounts of festive treats; and we send Christmas cards to our closest friends, colleagues, and loved ones.

For the most part, the holiday season approaches in much the same way in the Steckle household. Kathy Steckle is a spectacular cook who makes what is probably the best Christmas pudding in the hemisphere. The six Steckle grandchildren actively participate in their respective class concerts and other school functions, and the entire family attends a host of community events and seasonal soirées.

This already demanding time is intensified by Paul's public schedule of constituent meetings, votes in the House of Commons, travels to Ottawa, media interviews, and the issuance of formal correspondence and circulars, including sending out Christmas cards.

Most people send out Christmas cards to a limited group of friends and family members. I would suggest that an average household would send out between 15 and 50 cards, annually. I know from personal experience that the 97 cards mailed from the McClinchey household, while important, are quite time consuming and labour intensive and often take a back-seat to the plethora of other time-sensitive tasks associated with the month of December.

Being a Member of Parliament is a vocation that causes one to interact routinely with countless people from all walks of life. From premiers and cabinet ministers to doctors, teachers and farmers, as constituents, colleagues, and business contacts, they all find their way onto Paul's Christmas card list—in 2004 it totalled a whopping 4,287 households and offices.

Constructing and maintaining a database of this magnitude is a demanding task. While the data-entry portion of that job is generally farmed out to staff in the office, Paul and Kathy are largely responsible for the collection and referral of the names and addresses of the people to whom they would like to send Christmas wishes. Moreover, once the draft list is completed, it is printed, and both Paul and Kathy personally review it for accuracy and appropriateness. At that point, usually in late November, final revisions are made, and mailing labels are produced.

Subsequent to that, the more than four thousand cards that have been specially designed by a constituent and locally printed are stuffed, sealed, stamped, and posted for delivery in early December. While this might sound simple enough, it most certainly is not.

Setting aside the politically correct "Christmas card versus holiday card" debate, and notwithstanding the numerous formal complaints routinely received from people who were outraged because there was a typo in their street address or because one spouse's name appeared in bold print while the other's did not, the Paul Steckle family Christmas card of 2004 was one of the most controversial ever issued.

Why was it controversial? Because it depicted Paul and Kathy Steckle, their two adult children and their respective spouses, and the six Steckle grandchildren, all dressed in blaze-orange hats and hunting gear, sitting on two four-wheel all-terrain vehicles in front of a cornfield, holding arrows and firearms.

This was not the first time that one of Paul's Christmas cards garnered negative attention in the media. In 1996 the photo on the front of the card depicted the Steckle family dressed in clothes covered with a red and white maple leaf print, with an actual Canadian flag in the background. The card also referenced a Bible verse.

This card, without a doubt, was not one of his best; still, it was surprising when the card was singled out by the *Hill Times* (a newspaper circulated on Parliament Hill) as one of the most unattractive cards of the season. Furthermore, to have a family portrait publicly mocked in this manner is just another example of how politicians and their families need very thick skin if they are to survive the blunt and seemingly relentless barbs of a jaded populace and media.

It is normal practice for many parliamentary tasks to be routinely undertaken by staff in the name of the respective member of Parliament. In Paul's office this might include correspondence, casework, or public outreach, to name just a few examples. But Paul and Kathy view the Christmas card as something personal. Each year, they personally select an appropriate greeting and biblical verse, arrange a family portrait, and collect updated signatures from their children and grandchildren for insertion into the finished product.

Since his very first card, Paul has endeavoured to make the cover picture distinctive, showing his family in a state of togetherness. Aside from the obvious challenges posed by trying to convince 12 people, including very young children, to stand for a formal picture, there is the added complication of selecting a theme. With a young and growing family, taking the picture far in advance was simply not an option. More often than not, given tight time restrictions, the picture could not be taken during the winter, and as such an outdoor winter or Christmas theme was both impractical and logistically impossible. Therefore, other options were needed.

In 2004 the controversial photograph with the Steckles dressed in hunting gear was taken in October. In total, Paul's offices received approximately 335 complaints about the card, compared to more than 2500 compliments. The complaints, delivered by telephone, letter, e-mail, and fax, ranged from the measured to the unexpected and bizarre. Paul's Ottawa office received 573 e-mails on the subject, the vast majority of which were positive. I have transcribed excerpts from a selection of those e-mails below:

> I would like to thank you very much for the beautiful Christmas card. It was greatly appreciated … It is very nice to see your family enjoying the fruits of our rural way of life. My mother-in-law is seventy-plus years old and after seeing our card, [she] tried to steal [it.] Keep up the good work.
> —Signed by a family of four from Parry Sound, Ontario

> When reading Frank Etherington's December 27 column, "Gun-Toting MP Needs Shot of Reality on Gun Deaths," I found myself constantly checking the calendar. Surely I had not slept in until April 1. To my dismay, however, I soon discovered that it was indeed not April Fool's Day but just another example of a journalist ranting about a subject on which he is sadly uninformed or perhaps misinformed at best. Beyond the frankly shameful burst of ad hominem attacks on both Paul Steckle and the millions of responsible firearms owners across Canada, one can only be astounded that anyone with any sort of intellect would stand up and defend the abomination that is the current gun laws in Canada. Might I suggest that Etherington take some time out of his busy schedule devouring misinformation from the anti-gun lobby and head out to a local gun club to get the real story?
> —Signed by a male from Springfield, Ontario

> Just a quick note of our thoughts about the concerns towards your Christmas postcards you have sent out this year. It is wonderful to see a family as close as yours in today's society that obviously spends quality time together doing something they enjoy. I know your boys a little bit

from working in the same area together in business for the last 10 years, and they are very well respected and have a very good name in the business community. In closing we support your family togetherness and wish you the very best.

—Signed by a husband and wife from Grand Bend, Ontario

It is refreshing to see a family photo such as yours. It is obvious you have a close-knit family who enjoy the great outdoors. I truly and sincerely thank you for having the guts to send this out to the Canadian public. Hopefully, the guns/bow/arrows will show the people [that] Canada does have a safe firearms culture that is to be enjoyed by all and not demonized by the firearm registry and anti gun lobby.

—Signed by a male from Winnipeg, Manitoba

Just wanted to send you a quick note to support you and yours for trying to point out to the general public that not all gun owners are neanderthalic [sic] criminals ... I applaud your stance against the long rifle registration that has done nothing but cost us taxpayers money that could be better spent elsewhere. Now, if only some other Liberal MPs would start showing some spine. (Hell, I'd even be happy if they showed some common sense!)

—Signed by a male from Dartmouth, Nova Scotia

First time I've ever contacted a politician ... I just had to tell you that I loved the Christmas card. I applaud you for showing your family in a moment that applies to your own personal lives, rather than with the standard, stereotypical photo. You've also done a great job responding to criticism in the media ...

—Signed by a male from Komoka, Ontario

Thank you for this very Canadian family Christmas card. You have our vote; and backing if you ever decide to "run" for the PM's job.

—Signed by a husband and wife from Goderich, Ontario

I've been reading about your family's Christmas card caper, and all I can say is "keep up the good work." Don't let the politically correct, gun-hating, marriage-redefining, urban nitwits get you down.

—Signed by a male from North Bay, Ontario

The passion was even more intense (and often quite personal and plain nasty) on the other side of the issue—those who felt that the card was inappropriate—and many sought to unearth the alleged subliminal messaging that was intended when the Steckle family crafted the card.

> I recently read an article in the *Ottawa Citizen* about your Christmas card to constituents. I was a bit surprised at the theme of hunting in camouflage in a corn field ... I do find the choice of a picture depicting guns as part of a Christmas message unusual and lacking sensitivity to 50 per cent of the population of your constituency who live without full regard for their human rights—women who are abused and murdered on a daily basis, often by men whom they know ...
> —Signed by a male from Tiverton, Ontario

> We are writing to let you know how appalled we were by the Christmas card you sent us. We do not understand the point you were trying to make ... With global warming already affecting our climate, promoting the use of ATVs for entertainment purposes is shameful ... This card will not be displayed on our mantle ...
> —Signed by a husband and wife from Clinton, Ontario

> I cannot believe the levels that you will sink! You have turned Christmas into a redneck's paradise. Guns have no place in a civilized society, and I am ashamed to know an MP that would showcase them like this.
> —Submitted anonymously

> This so-called Christmas card shows your clear hatred towards women. These guns are used to kill women and now you promote them to kids.
> —Signed by a woman from Beaverbank, Nova Scotia

> I can excuse the fact that you like to hunt, and I can forgive the fact that you voted against gun control, but now this is the line. For you to put out such propaganda in favour of the Iraq war is unexcusable [sic]. I have had enough ... My wife and our three children will be voting for the NDP next time. You are finished in government."
> —Submitted anonymously

> Stop pushing your religious values on me. I do not need to receive a taxpayer-funded church sermon from my Member of Parliament. The

Charter of Rights gives me and all Canadians freedom of religion, and I would ask you to respect that. If you can't, might I suggest that [you] call up the Reform Party and ask to join them. You are not a liberal, so stop saying that you are.

—Signed by a man from Willowbrook, Saskatchewan

I don't know what to say. This card is a disgrace to Canada. Children without helmets on motor vehicles are a bad example for others. I also understand that you are not even wearing hunter orange. This is another bad example for others … you should be ashamed and resign.

—Signed by a man from Bois-des-Filion, Quebec

Aw, how cute. Yeap, guns and Christmas always seem to go together, now don't they just? Gee, for a minute I thought I was looking at a group of redneck gun-loving right-wing religious-nut Republicans from the "Jesus" states of the United States of America, but nooooo, it's our own dysfunctional northern rednecks. Just one question? How come your women are fat? Get them out in those fields hunting to burn off some calories, come on, get with the program, laughs and laughs and laughs, … You all have a gun Merry Christmas, ya hear?

—Submitted by a woman (no address provided)

While these are only a few of the responses generated by the media spotlight, the overall viciousness of the entire spectacle far surpassed anything that I would have expected. In some cases the card seemed to inspire hope, while in other cases it sparked absolute furor. Regardless, the Steckle family had no hidden motives when they prepared the card. They simply wanted to showcase the fact that their family enjoys certain outdoor pursuits and each other's company on December 25 and every day of the year. In a day when the country faced countless serious and pressing matters of national concern, for a simple Christmas card to ignite such a display was telling, to say the least.

In his own defence, Paul had a conversation with *London Free Press* reporter Ian Gillespie:

Reporter: Although MP Paul Steckle is holding a gun, I
                       think he's the sitting duck … The Liberal MP for
                       Huron-Bruce has raised eyebrows with his family

Christmas card, which depicts the Steckle clan bedecked in camouflage and brandishing firearms and bows and arrows.

Paul: [The card] was never done with an intent to raise an issue. My wife is the one who designs the Christmas cards. We've done it for 11 years, and every year we have a different venue. One year we did the patriotism one, where we dressed in red and white ... so we'd look like we were celebrating Canada Day. [This year] I'm chairman of the Standing Committee on Agriculture. What better way to depict where I come from? I'm a rural guy.

Reporter: The outspoken MP, who leans so far right one wonders how he avoids toppling out of the Liberal tower, says the card has irked both city and country dwellers.

Paul: People say it doesn't represent Christmas. Well, the generic cards that Parliament Hill puts out don't tell a Christmas story, either. In fact, many of them don't even use the word Christmas. They use Happy Holidays and all sorts of generic terms.

At this juncture, the reporter, who was clearly no fan of Paul's stand on such matters, offered the following closing notion, which I believe summarized the reason for the Christmas card hullabaloo:

Now, I'm sure many readers are rolling their eyes at this point. But not me. I disagree with many of Steckle's political views. And I don't hunt. But in this case, I think his family is just another victim of the ever-widening war between urban and rural residents. I think it's the height of hypocrisy when a bunch of self-righteous, SUV-driving, meat-loving urbanites routinely demean and dismiss their rural cousins. I doubt Steckle would've been criticized if his card depicted a family of golfers. Ironically, with their water waste, pesticides, and poor land use, ill-planned golf courses likely cause more environmental damage than many duck hunters. If you ask me, the Steckles are just easy targets for city simpletons who wouldn't know a silo from a soybean—but are convinced they hold the moral high ground.

It turned out that while the Steckle family Christmas card of 2004 was never intended to be a provocative political or social statement, it underscored an expanding cultural problem that Canadians, particularly rural Canadians, needed—and still need—to address if they are to survive long term.

While more than 60 per cent of Canada's population lives within the six largest cities of this country, there is also a diverse and robust culture that exists and flourishes outside of those select urban centres. Furthermore, while Canadians living in the rural regions of the country are, from a population perspective, fewer in number than their urban cousins, they are no less important to the overall fiscal and cultural triumphs and failures of Canada as a whole. In short, farmers feed cities, and rural Canadians support our agrarian base. Some urban dwellers have conveniently forgotten this fact and, as such, a rural/urban divide has developed. It would seem to me that any good rural member of Parliament would be duty-bound to expose this reality. If that is the case, mission accomplished, and Merry Christmas.

Chapter 17

One More Last Chance

I guess this is good-bye. I've had enough bullshit. Does Paul Martin honestly think that we believe he knew nothing of millions of dollars being siphoned off for political cronies? And does he think he can continue to bully constituents out of politics to suit his own whims? That greasy Wop Valeri might have won Hamilton East, but it came at a price—I've cast my last Liberal vote. Enough is enough. This is good-bye.

> —An e-mail to Paul Steckle, signed by a Ripley man,
> received during the writ (campaign) period

The election campaign of 2005/2006 was perhaps the most vicious and spiteful of any national campaign conducted since 1993. The four primary national party leaders permitted the debate to digress to the point that name-calling, personal slurs, and accusations of criminal misdeeds replaced real policy discussion and debate as headline news. The media seemed all too happy to enter the fray. They engaged in a frenzy of reporting, the style and tone of which is usually reserved for the tabloids at the grocery store. On a local level, even Paul Steckle conceded that the mood was "nasty" as he moved throughout the streets and back roads of the constituency. The malevolent and ferocious nature of the election battle was most assuredly the culmination of a slide in decorum that had permeated into nearly every facet of national governance during the preceding two years. Everyone was angry, everyone was depressed, and everyone wanted election day to arrive yesterday, already.

The election itself was called by the newly recruited governor general, at the request of Prime Minister Paul Martin, following the November 28, 2005, Commons vote of no confidence in the Liberal government. The vote, which was widely anticipated, topped off months of parliamentary debate that had been anything but parliamentary. On the morning of November 29, 2005, the guesswork, speculation, and partisan brinkmanship were over, and the campaign was underway in earnest. MPs, their staff, and political pundits alike boarded planes, trains, and busses, evacuating Ottawa for the Christmas election that none of them seemed to really want. Given that the campaign was to extend over Christmas and New Year's Day, the writ period, which is usually around 36 days in duration, was to be nearly 8 weeks long. Prime Minister Martin had opted for a 57-day campaign. Strategically speaking, the Liberal Party believed that the longer campaign would provide them with the time they needed to expose Stephen Harper as a scary and devious personality, a tactic that had been successfully employed in the 2004 election campaign. While that impulse may have been sound on paper, the approach was far less effective in real life.

On the front lines, securing volunteers was difficult, due to the traditional holiday rush and winter vacations. Snowbirds wanted no part of any political campaign as they prepared themselves for their annual winter migration. And soliciting political donations at Christmas meant competing with worthy and necessary charitable groups, such as the Christmas Bureau and the local hospitals, churches, and food banks. All in all, it seemed as though political leaders had given little or no consideration to the impact that an election would have on the lives of citizens during a time of year that should have been reserved for family and community endeavours. Furthermore, much of Canada is impassable during the winter months, and for the balance of the country, particularly in the snow belt of southern Ontario, winter road conditions are a gamble, at best.

As if this wasn't enough, the national Liberal campaign team seemed to stumble from one crisis to the next, bereft of any obvious plan or overall line of attack. The Liberal "war room" was in disarray, and individual campaigns were discouraged and angry. Aside from an almost total absence of nationally produced campaign materials, promotional items, or platform documents, the lack of a coherent rural and agricultural policy helped to highlight the fact that commodity prices were severely depressed and that the average Canadian farmer was facing his single greatest economic challenge in a generation. That, when coupled with off-the-cuff and ill-begotten talk of eliminating the Notwithstanding Clause of the Constitution; the fumbled, ever-changing, and poorly communicated proposal of a national handgun ban; and the much-touted, politically motivated and factually challenged RCMP Income Trust investigation of the finance minister was simply too much for the beleaguered Liberal Party machinery to endure. With every passing day, these issues, each in their own way, pummelled Liberal re-election efforts. In the dying days of the campaign, it seemed as though the fight was not about winning but about reducing the hemorrhaging as much as possible.

At the local level, the Paul Steckle campaign faced fallout too. Angry calls, voter apathy, scant volunteer availability, and a range of technical problems—such as an inability to secure telephone services—just added to a growing list of problems. Voter fatigue, notions of corruption and a media-driven desire for change nearly toppled the four-term, traditionally popular, incumbent MP. Day after day, the capable and dedicated Huron-Bruce Liberal team plodded away, quietly voicing their despair, their fears, and their exasperation with the situation from one end to the other.

Finally, election day, Monday, January 23, 2006, was upon us. The Huron-Bruce Liberal campaign team completed certain necessary, last-minute tasks before our headquarters operation transferred from Clinton to the Sacred Heart Roman Catholic Church Hall in Wingham. The band played and well-wishers looked on as radio, television, and print media reporters assembled from across the region in anticipation of the closing of the polls. Campaign spokespeople fanned out in an effort to recount, debate, and spin the results, whatever they would be. Scott Miller, the local A Channel reporter, suggested on air that the "incumbent MP Paul Steckle is facing one of the toughest battles of his career."[1] There was no denying a nervous feeling that change was in the air as guests began arriving. The stage was set, and at 8:00 PM, the tabulation of the results began.

By the time the polls officially closed, Paul and Kathy Steckle, along with their children, their children's spouses, and their grandchildren, had arrived at the home of Murray and Pat Gaunt. Murray Gaunt, the former area MPP, and his wife had agreed to host the Steckle family at their Wingham home as they watched the results come in. Paul would then have a chance to observe and absorb the results, both nationally and locally, in private before publicly commenting to the media or to supporters. In addition to the obvious benefit of solitude in the event of an electoral loss, being off-site also permitted Paul to make a more dramatic entrance at his campaign-appreciation party. While this was a practice that had been employed in each of Paul's previous federal campaigns, it was not until 2006 that the benefits were most fully realized.

Back at the Sacred Heart Roman Catholic Church Hall, it did not look good for the national Liberal team. Those in attendance were pressed to the television screens, mouths agape, as the results began to come in. First, the East Coast delivered an almost unblemished streak of Liberal red. While the congregation was observably pleased with the results, Quebec and Ontario promised to be the real battleground on which the outcome would rest. Then it happened: The Conservatives began to capture seats in Quebec. For the first time since their obliteration in 1993, the Conservative Party was a factor in central Canada. It was expected that the Bloc Québécois would recapture several seats, but as Conservative victories were declared, it seemed that a sweep might be in the cards. Ontario delivered more of the same, although the Liberal Party dominated the seat-rich Greater Toronto Area (GTA). As each of the neighbouring ridings in the region was painted Conservative blue, it became apparent that the numbers in Huron-Bruce would be closer than anyone had anticipated.

---

1. Scott Miller, (the A Channel News), on location at the Paul Steckle election night volunteer gathering in Wingham, Ontario, January 23, 2006.

Margaret and Rick McInroy, the Liberal scrutineers placed in the Huron-Bruce Elections Canada office, began reporting via cell phone to the campaign designates in Wingham. Kevin Wilbee, a Walton-area youth, monitored incoming information and Web updates every few seconds, posting them for all to review. An eager crowd gathered as the results were displayed.

By 11:30 PM, more than three hours after the first results had been received, Ben Lobb, the Conservative candidate was leading Paul Steckle by 12 votes. As the results vacillated, the assembled crowed cheered and jeered accordingly. If nothing else, it made for an adrenaline-filled few hours, with random supporters conducting live radio and television interviews between the electoral updates. At approximately 11:32 PM, the campaign manager's cell phone rang with the news that had been anticipated all night: The scrutineers from the 23 polls in Southampton and Port Elgin had just delivered their results. Paul Steckle had won all but three polls—and that meant that he had just won the 39th general election. The celebrations began.

A few moments later, Paul Steckle, his wife, and his family arrived to a frenzied room of supporters and media representatives. The mood was jubilant among supporters but frantic among some of the reporters. Near scuffles broke out as campaign staff attempted to restrain and systematize certain media reporters so as to schedule organized interviews, but when the dust settled, the newly re-elected Paul Steckle commented on the Liberal defeat and the new Conservative minority government: "The country wanted change and their votes reflected that ... All candidates who ran should be commended because it was a gruelling campaign."[2] Paul went on to thank his family and his supporters for once again renewing their faith in him, even if the plurality was reduced.

In the end, of the 53,546 votes cast, Paul Steckle squeaked by with 21,260, the Conservatives received 20,289, the NDP received 8,689, and the balance was split between rejected ballots and the three fringe contes-

2. Paul Steckle, MP, in a speech to Liberal supporters at the election night volunteer gathering in Wingham, Ontario, January 23, 2006.

tants. Nationally, Stephen Harper was elected as the 22nd prime minister of Canada, and outgoing Prime Minister Paul Martin, while doing much better overall than originally anticipated, was reduced to the position of leader of the Official Opposition. Unfortunately, as is the custom after such events, Paul Martin announced that he would retain his seat as an MP but that he would resign as party leader. In a nationally televised statement to his supporters, Martin said, "When I think about it, 17 years is a long time, and you have stood by me ... I will always be at the service of the party ... We acted on the belief that Canada is strongest as a nation when we endeavoured to ensure that no Canadian is ever left behind ... It is a privilege to serve Canada."[3]

With that, it seemed as though the election that nobody really wanted was finally over. In politics, however, nothing is ever quite what it might appear. The next morning on CKNX's *The Talk Show*, on which Paul had been invited to discuss the previous night's events, the recently defeated Conservative candidate again renewed the unsubstantiated public speculation that Paul intended to cross the floor to sit with the new government's caucus. This was a recurring and false rumour that had most recently appeared in the April 12, 2005, edition of the *London Free Press*. In response to that report, Paul issued a media communiqué that stated, in part, "I was tremendously surprised to learn that I am considering a run at the Conservative nomination. I hope they understand that I don't even vote for them." In the same release Paul Steckle went on to say, "Aside from the fact that I have been a Liberal since 1968, I have no intention of walking away from a party and a leader that has a record of monumental achievements. This party, like all parties, has its faults, but I will never cross over to an organization that counts Brian Mulroney as one of its most ardent supporters."[4] Paul simply chose to laugh at the matter because he knew that he had no intention of crossing the floor to the Conservative

---

3. Rt. Hon. Paul Martin, PC, MP, Prime Minister of Canada, in a nationally televised speech to Liberal supporters in the riding of LaSalle-Émard, Quebec, January 23, 2006.
4. Paul Steckle, MP, in a press release issued to Huron-Bruce print media, April 12th, 2005.

or any other partisan group. Had he really wanted to leave the Liberal Party, he would have done so years earlier, when the local Canadian Alliance Riding Association (the forerunner to the current Conservative Party) approached him about running in Huron-Bruce as their candidate against the Chrétien Liberals of the day.

The next duty for Paul Steckle was the official swearing-in ceremony. Under Canadian law, once the election results are properly certified by the chief electoral officer in Ottawa, he is required to then relay that certification to the clerk of the House of Commons. An MP-elect must then affirm an oath of office and sign the roll as a member of the Canadian House of Commons, a distinction that is valid and binding for the life of the Parliament. The unpretentious ceremony, which is officiated by the clerk of the House of Commons or a designate, is the same as it has been for generations past. The Oath of Allegiance reads simply: "I, (Paul Daniel Steckle), do swear that I will be faithful, and bear true allegiance to Her Majesty Queen Elizabeth the Second, Her Heirs and Successors, according to Law, so help me God." Paul's fifth installation ceremony was held on February 24, 2006, and was witnessed by a large number of family, friends, supporters, and well-wishers that included his wife, Kathy; Rick and Margaret McInroy; Sandy Hamamoto; Nick and Joan Whyte; Geordie Palmer; Mervyn and Dawn Erb; Kathy Bromley; Howard Aitkin; Greg, Julie, and Mieka McClinchey; Mahlon and Pearl Ann Martin; Joe and Kathleen Semple; Cam Steckle; Glen and Donna Thiel; Joanne Flanagan; Steve Sharpe and his father; Amanda-Lynn Feeney; Allan Vander-Spek; Jim and Ruth Gingerich; Phil Erb; Fred Deichert; Ken and Margaret Caldwell; Jim and Jocelyn Hogg; Jean Denis Fréchette; Bibiane Ouellette; Chera Jelley; Cheryl Fougere; Gerry and Mary Kolz; Phil and Patricia Laporte; Wayne Clausius; and Gerald and Cathy Shantz, to name just a few. Those of us closest to Paul wanted to savour the victory because as with any minority government, there was no telling when the next campaign would be.

Paul Steckle's offices in Ottawa and Goderich opened on the morning of January 24, 2006, without missing a beat. Paul had a great deal that he wanted to tackle, and he insisted that no time be wasted. The close election results had, in many ways, made him slightly bitter, even as it seemed to energise him. The new government was scheduled to be sworn in on February 6, 2006, and Paul wanted to ensure that the farm-income crisis was the first order of business on the new government's agenda. To achieve this, when the new agriculture minister Chuck Strahl returned to his desk after being installed, he found Paul Steckle's letter. That correspondence, which was also sent to the new prime minister, read:

> I am writing so that I might underscore to you the dire situation facing Canadian agriculture; in particular, the primary producers engaged in the grains and oilseed sector. Furthermore, I would like to formally request a meeting with you at the earliest possible opportunity to discuss the Risk Management Programme (RMP), designed and proposed by the Ontario White Bean Producers' Marketing Board; the Ontario Canola Growers Association; the Ontario Coloured Bean Growers Association; the Ontario Corn Producers Association; the Ontario Soybean Growers; the Ontario Wheat Producers Marketing Board; and the Seed Corn Growers of Ontario. Your urgent action on this matter is crucial if we are to prevent the current farm-income crisis from intensifying and further weakening the overall economy of the industry and rural Canada. To be clear, I unreservedly support the RMP, and I am prepared to engage in immediate cooperative actions with you and your officials in an effort to make the RMP a rapid reality for our farmers. In the 39th general election, this issue was paramount in the riding of Huron-Bruce, a constituency that relies heavily upon the success of the agricultural sector. As a result, the Liberal Party offered complete support for the RMP proposal, and I will make every effort to ensure that this support is maintained. I am hopeful that your government will likewise endorse the RMP. Failure to act directly on the implementation of this producer-conceived program will result in devastating repercussions for our primary producers.

The local riding media picked up on the letter, and in a bizarre and unanticipated twist, Paul was subjected to public scorn for daring to make demands of the new minister. I suppose some local farmer leaders expected that Paul would roll over and play dead just because he was no longer on the government benches. Paul, however, fired back in an effort to show that he was not neutralized; he was still the MP for Huron-Bruce, and he intended to take his duties seriously. The time period following the election of January 2006 was busier than ever. Paul was no longer just another rural member on a bench of dozens. He was now a five-term, senior political voice. His opinions were sought out, and he found himself playing a leadership role in a party desperate for renewal. He was one of the only truly rural Liberal MPs in the House of Commons, and he was already quite experienced at Opposition tactics. Paul was now in the role for which he had trained during the entire course of his life and career, and he was relishing every second of it.

In the 12-month period between January 2006 and January 2007, Paul Steckle:

- was directly responsible for the introduction of Bill C-338, the first real piece of anti-abortion legislation to appear in the House of Commons for nearly two decades;

- was elected as the vice chair of the Standing Committee on Agriculture and Agri-Food;

- was asked to serve as the Ontario campaign chair for a Liberal leadership campaign;

- oversaw the research, drafting, and release of a widely accepted and comprehensive rural and agriculture policy discussion paper;

- functioned as one of only nine caucus members who supported Stéphane Dion's successful leadership bid from the beginning;

- initiated and focused a national debate on the appropriateness of lowering the Peace Tower flag to honour fallen Canadian soldiers, subsequent to the death of Corporal Matthew Dinning;

- singularly pressed for the creation of a rural affairs critic post for the Official Opposition

- helped to sway the Liberal Party to alter its national policy framework in a way that would call upon the government to establish a rural affairs minister and a National Agriculture Policy and to implement the producer-conceived Risk Management Program.

Without question, Paul Steckle hit his stride in the Thirty-ninth Parliament of Canada in a way that many never expected. This 64-year-old farmer-turned-legislator clearly proved that politics is a game in which having heart can make all the difference. Some people may find themselves languishing after many years at the same routine job, but Paul seems to draw strength and energy from an unseen source. He has the experience of a senior statesman, the instincts of a partisan, and the energy of a 40-year-old. While there is no telling how long his tenure in office will last, until then, his constituents, the people of Huron-Bruce, and his colleagues in the Parliament of Canada should watch this MP very closely.

Chapter 18

Vermächtnis

I have always said that there are two great callings in life. One, the religious life or service to God. And two, serving your fellow man or public service ... Democracy works ... You can make a difference.

—Right Honourable John Napier Turner
In an address to the 2006 Liberal Party of Canada Leadership
Convention, Montreal
December 2, 2006

It was about mid-morning on Saturday, December 17, 2005. The weather had been wet and miserable for most of the month, so the election campaign had been slow going. The Liberal Party had been assailed on nearly every possible front, and it seemed as though the electoral contest would never end. I had just hung up the phone from yet another nasty confrontation with Bell Canada over some technical problems with phone services that the campaign headquarters had experienced. I swung around in my chair, reached for my coffee cup, and saw Sandy Hamamoto, Paul's Deputy Campaign Manager, coming towards me. Sandy and I had both committed to suspending our duties—and our pay—in Paul's office in favour of working full time on the campaign. That meant seven days a week in the bear pit. Sandy had left her friends, her routine and the comfort of her regular surroundings in Ottawa for the scattered life of a political hack, living out of a suitcase and enduring strange hours in the cold, wet and seemingly despondent grind of a Christmas writ period. I, after leaving my wife and then 18-day-old baby girl, Mieka, to fend for themselves, set up temporary residence at the makeshift office in Clinton. In short, we sat at the helm of a federal election campaign effort, having suspended our personal lives and financial interests for nearly two months over the holiday season.

Now, Sandy saw fit to break the unspoken rule that coffee comes first, conversation second. She announced that someone was in the front office, asking to speak with me. (She named him, but let's just say his name was "Bill.") I took that sip of coffee, and then pulled myself off my chair and headed towards the front door. After exchanging pleasantries, Bill and I sat down at my desk (actually a folding table) to talk.

I had met this McKillop Township man on a number of occasions, dating back several years. In my capacity with Paul's office in Goderich, I had provided assistance to Bill or received feedback from him on about a half-dozen occasions in the past. He was his usual quiet and unassuming self, but an impromptu meeting or a cold call during a campaign can bring the unexpected.

Bill said that he had been in the coffee shop, where the guys had been talking about the election. Some were happy with Paul, and some were not. He knew that Paul was doing what he could for the farmers, but he also knew that Paul could not do it alone. He then slid a ten-page document across the desk. It was a project that his daughter "Erica" had prepared for school, titled, "Backbenchers are more than just voting machines." He said that he thought that it was "really good," and he was hoping that Paul might read it; perhaps, Bill suggested, it would help Paul to figure out another way to do things in Ottawa. Bill went on to point out that in our system of government, backbench MPs have real power, if they opt to use it. We talked for about 30 minutes, and then I committed to reading the paper and sharing it with Paul. I stuffed the document in my briefcase and hurried out the door to my next appointment.

That was the last I thought about the matter until about 11:30 PM, when it popped back into my head as I drove home from my last engagement of the day. In an effort to clear the decks in anticipation for the rigours of the next morning, I diverted back to the office in Clinton, where I took the paper out of my briefcase and read it. The opening line read, "Members of Parliament, who sit as backbenchers of the House of Commons, are often seen as a voting machine; this is not the case." From that point on this young girl outlined how MPs have tremendous power if they would only realize it and exercise it. In a no-nonsense, forthright, and to-the-point dissection of Canadian governance, Erica outlined with simplistic clarity what Paul Steckle had taught me over the course of more than a decade—that the real power is not in the front row; it is in the hands of those who sit in the chairs behind them. If citizens would vote for the best person on a ballot, not necessarily for the perceptions of the party with which they have aligned themselves, parliamentary governance would work much better. Erica also observed that some backbenchers don't aspire for cabinet portfolios; they just want to be the best local MP that they can be. Most importantly, she used Paul Steckle as a prime example of this kind of thinking.

While it may seem like a small thing, I thought that her point was anything but peripheral minutia. Leave it to a young child to see past the spin and the bias in which we often find ourselves embroiled. She managed to sum up Paul Steckle's legacy to Parliament, to Canada, and to the people of Huron-Bruce in just a few simple words.

When Paul Steckle was first elected to federal office in 1993, the thought of a governing representative voting against his or her party was almost unthinkable. For example, when the Mulroney government sought to pass the Goods and Services Tax (GST) into law in the late 1980s, no one was surprised when then Huron-Bruce MP Murray Cardiff voted in favour of the measure. As the representative of the people of Huron-Bruce, he voted to implement a tax that was overwhelmingly loathed by the majority of the people that he was paid to represent. It seemed like a paradox, but for generations, that is exactly how the system worked. Then, along came Paul Steckle, with his radical notions that an MP should be the voice *of* the people and not the voice *to* the people. No one had bothered to tell Paul that tradition dictated that he should vote how he was told to vote; Paul would not be a trained seal. The notions of democracy in the face of a determined and capable party whip were not just casually espoused values; Paul was actually prepared to put up, rather than shut up; he was going to do exactly as he said he would do. The result of his shocking behaviour hit the national stage like an atomic blast.

In the early days, Paul's lack of adherence to occasional vacillations in prescribed party policy (as determined by the leader of the day and/or non-elected officials) caused local partisans to scream foul. Political observers and certain media pundits predicted that the parliamentary system would collapse into a state of political anarchy if the trend continued or expanded into common practice. They labelled Paul as a maverick and a malcontent. Prime Minister Chrétien himself called Paul "ungrateful," as if Paul's electoral victories were the sole result of Mr. Chrétien's intervention and not the result of the electorate responding to an MP with a sound constituency focus. Despite the dire warnings of chaos and systemic pandemonium, one member voting against his own party turned to three, which turned to nine, and eventually to twenty-one and more. The oddity of the new political reality is that nothing bad happened. The sky did not fall and the Government of Canada was not mired in bedlam. To the contrary, in the last term of the Paul Martin Liberal administration, there was talk of the "democratic deficit"; local government was empowered; parliamentary committees vetted cabinet appointments; Standing Committee chairs were elected, rather than the postings being filled by decree of the party brass; and MPs and parliamentary secretaries were afforded new and far-reaching powers to devise legislation and policy and to exercise oversight.

More recently, emboldened by the new liberties commonly and openly exercised by the elected caucus, the Liberal Party rank-and-file selected a leader, Stéphane Dion, who was not the obvious "anointed" one. He did not have the support of the traditional party power brokers, and for the first time in history, the Liberal Party elected a leader who was not widely favoured or in first place during the lead-up to the leadership convention. The result was a leader-elect who owed nothing to anyone; someone who had a free hand to select those he needed from a limitless pool of talent.

He was able to strip away the deadwood, as he did not need to pay back the loyalty or support of the establishment, nor was he beholden to or caught up in past leadership battles. From where I sit, that seems like evolution breeding true, healthy, and peaceful internal transformation within a profession that typically resists wholesale change in nearly every conceivable fashion.

I am suggesting that Paul Steckle's true legacy may not be as much about what he delivered in the short term as it is about what he has delivered—and will continue to deliver—in the long term. Sure, he secured additional funding for invasive-species control in the Great Lakes. He helped to eliminate the Notional Input Tax Credit. He fought to protect and preserve a healthy and robust rural way of life. He worked to promote real legislative reform on cruelty to animals. And he tackled hundreds of individual injustices during his tenure in office. But sadly, in 50 years no one will remember, and worse yet, no one will care. Should I be fortunate enough to be on this earth 50 years from now, however, I am confident that Paul's contributions will be more readily apparent, even if time itself has rendered his personal role inert or forgotten.

Chinese philosopher Lau-tzo said that the journey of a thousand miles begins with a single step. Looking back, that first step—his speaking honestly, frankly, and without regard for how his superiors might reprimand or reward him—was Paul Steckle's first stride towards bringing a measure of true accountability and indisputable democracy to this constitutional monarchy that we call Canada. By throwing open the doors to the notion that MPs are the voice of the people, not partisan servants who must blindly follow orders, Paul helped to blow off the cobwebs that had formed in and around the great institutions of this great country. By placing the needs of his community ahead of his personal ambitions, he has denied himself the legal title of "honourable" (by declining to accept a promotion—including an appointment to the Privy Council of Canada) but gained the praiseworthy reputation for frankness and integrity.

I feel it's worth reiterating that I have had the distinct pleasure of knowing and working alongside Paul Steckle for more than 13 years. I have come to see him as outgoing, yet shy; as honest, yet cunning; as aggressive, yet kind-hearted; as traditional, yet progressive; and as stubborn, yet mal-leable. I find it ironic—even bizarre—that a conservative-minded tradi-tionalist Mennonite would be a force for change. Setting aside his old-school attitudes on certain issues, Paul, when viewed in the grander context, was—and continues to be—dynamic and avant-garde.

Just as tall trees are known by their shadows, so are good men known by their enemies. Paul has most assuredly secured enemies during his 30 years in elected life, but he also has endeared himself to many. Although I have heard many negative comments about him, I have seen the real Paul Steckle—the small boy who was certain that he could make a cement boat float; the private family man; the ambitious and aspiring young Liberal; the dedicated municipal politician; and the determined and resolute MP. Each of these incarnations remains part of Paul and, for better or worse, has made him what he is today. Regardless of one's personal political stripe or viewpoints, few would quibble over the profound impact that Paul has had on federal politics in Canada and in Huron-Bruce.

It is my fondest wish that regardless of their partisan affiliation, his suc-cessors will demonstrate that same temperament, moral fibre, and integ-rity. It is a rare quality, but it is one that I am convinced can take root in the difficult and often rocky soil that fills the halls of Parliament.

Paul Steckle, MP
Huron-Bruce (Ontario)
Biography

Since first being elected Member of Parliament for Huron-Bruce in 1993 and subsequently in 1997, 2000, 2004, and 2006, Paul Steckle has balanced his time between his parliamentary duties and his obligations as a husband, father, and grandfather. Paul and his wife, Kathy (née Erb), live on the Stanley Township farm where Paul was born in 1942. They are active members of the Zurich Mennonite Church and enjoy taking part in community activities with their two sons Cameron and Brian (and Kathy and Bonnie, their respective wives) and their six grandchildren (Brent, Shawn, Valerie, Dylan, Devon, and Darren).

LIBERAL CAUCUS ACTIVITIES (1993–2007)

- National Liberal Caucus

- Ontario Caucus

- South-western and Southern Ontario Caucus

- Rural Caucus, Treasurer

- Outdoors Caucus, Treasurer

- Elected Co-Chair of Rural Caucus Committee

- Feather Caucus

- Dairy Caucus

- Gasoline Caucus

- Auto Caucus

STANDING AND CAUCUS COMMITTEE MEMBERSHIP (1993–2007)

- Caucus Committee of the Environment and Economic Sustainability

- Standing Committee on Agriculture and Agri-Food (Chair 2003–2005)

- Vice Chair, Standing Committee on Fisheries and Oceans

- Vice Chair, Standing Committee on Agriculture and Agri-Food

- Standing Committee on Fisheries and Oceans

- Standing Committee on the Environment

- Standing Committee on the Parliamentary Library

- Sub-Committee on Agriculture and Agri-Food: Western Grain Transportation

- Associate Member of the Standing Committee on Agriculture and Agri-Food

- Democratic Deficit Committee

- Liberal Caucus Committee on Gasoline Pricing

PARLIAMENTARY MEMBERSHIPS AND AFFILIATIONS (1993–2007)

- Liberal Rural Caucus Treasurer

- Liberal Outdoors Caucus Treasurer

- Canada–Taiwan Parliamentary Association

- Canada–UK Inter-Parliamentary Association

- Canada–Japan Inter-Parliamentary Association

- Canada–Germany Inter-Parliamentary Association

- Canada–Ireland Inter-Parliamentary Association

- Canada–Italy Inter-Parliamentary Association

- Canada–Russia Inter-Parliamentary Association

- Canada–Africa Parliamentary Association

- Canada–Europe Parliamentary Association

- Canada–Cuba Parliamentary Friendship Group

- Chair, National Prayer Breakfast

- Chair, Parliamentary Prayer Breakfast

- Co-Chair, Parliamentary Pro-Life Caucus

REPORTS PREPARED (1993–2007)

- Technology vs. Tradition (Herbal Medicine/Methods)

- E.I. Reform in the Face of a Growing Surplus

- Finances of the Nation (a Post-Deficit Era)

- Directions for Canadian Youth (a Huron-Bruce Perspective)

- Social Security Reform (a Huron-Bruce Perspective)

- Future Direction for Canadian Agriculture (a Huron-Bruce Perspective)

- Signatory–Liberal Caucus Report on the Future of the Financial Service Sector

- Signatory–Liberal Caucus Report on Gasoline Pricing

- From the Arm Chair to the Committee Chair (Future of Healthcare)

- Rural Canada: Sharing the wealth beyond tomorrow

LIBERAL PARTY AFFILIATION (1967–2007)

- Associate Critic for Agriculture and Agri-Food (2006–2007)

- Leadership Campaign Worker for the Hon. Stéphane Dion

- Leadership Campaign Worker for the Rt. Hon. Paul Martin

- Leadership Campaign Worker for the Rt. Hon. Jean Chrétien

- Delegate to All LPC National Leadership Conventions

- Leadership Campaign Worker for the Hon. Paul Hellyer

- President of the Huron Young Liberal Association

POLITICAL (MUNICIPAL) CAREER NOTES

- Provincial Representative on Board of Health

- Member of the Huron County Health Board

- Warden of Huron County

- Reeve of Stanley Township

- Member of the Huron County Council

- Member of the Stanley Township Council

NON-POLITICAL CAREER NOTES/COMMUNITY INVOLVEMENT

- Farmer (mixed pork/cash crop)

- Sales: CG Farm Supply, Zurich–Case Industrial Division

- Member of the Ausable-Bayfield Conservation Authority

- Member of the Ontario Federation of Anglers and Hunters

- Past President of the Huron County Farm Safety Association

- Past Member of the Huron County Pork Producers

- Member of the Bluewater Rest Home Board of Directors

- Pilot

Paul Steckle, MP, Huron-Bruce
Room 484 Confederation Building
House of Commons
Ottawa, Ontario, K1A 0A6
(613) 992-8234/steckp0@parl.gc.ca/(613) 995-6350 fax

Pictures

Every Member of Parliament is afforded countless opportunities to create and expand a vast personal photo album. Paul Steckle's collection contains literally hundreds of interesting pictures. The following represent a sampling of that collection.

(Above) An 18-year-old Paul Steckle sports the clean-cut profile of an MP in
waiting (1960).
(Below) The newly married couple, Paul and Kathy Steckle (June 26, 1965).

(Above) Paul (back row—standing second from the right) poses with his father and mother, his siblings, and their growing extended family (1967).
(Below) The three Steckle children, Cameron, Connie and Brian, anxiously await the chance to see what Santa delivered (December 25, 1971).

(Above) Paul and Kathy Steckle pose as a family with their three children, Cameron, Brian, and Connie (July 1973; three months before Connie's tragic death in a farming accident).
(Below) Paul and Kathy say hello to the 1970s.

(Above) Left to right, standing: Kathy Steckle (Paul's wife); Seleda Steckle (Paul's mother); Shawn Steckle (Paul's grandson); Cameron Steckle (Paul's son); Kathy Steckle (Cameron's wife); Bonnie Steckle (Brian's wife); Brian Steckle (Paul's son); Robert Marleau (the clerk of the House of Commons). Seated: Paul Steckle, with Brent Steckle (Paul's grandson), during the ceremony of Paul's first swearing in as the MP for Huron-Bruce (1993).

(Above) In 1995, Paul and Kathy Steckle are received at 24 Sussex Drive (the official residence of the Prime Minister of Canada) by Prime Minister Chrétien and his wife, Aline.

(Above) Paul Steckle addresses the First Session of the 35th Parliament (1994), as his elected Liberal colleagues listen and look on.

(Above) Paul Steckle takes a moment for a photo with Liberal supporters and campaign workers during his 1997 re-election campaign kick-off. Left to right: Paul Steckle, Darlene Vincent, Rick McInroy, and Margaret McInroy.

(Above and Below) The extended Steckle family has changed over the years but continues to enjoy their time together.

Meeting and conversing with interesting and unique world figures is an important
part of being a member of Canada's Parliament.
(Above) Paul Steckle meets with His Majesty King Abdullah II of Jordan, as
senator Gildas Molgat looks on (1999).
(Below) Prime Minister Chrétien introduces Paul and Kathy Steckle to Her
Majesty Queen Elizabeth the Second and H.R.H. Prince Philip, the Duke of
Edinburgh, at the state dinner in Toronto (Royal York Hotel, June 28, 1997).

(Above) Paul Steckle shares a laugh in the Commons Chamber with a friend and personal supporter, Bob Baker (2005).
(Below) Paul conducts a personal tour on the House of Commons floor with a group of Huron-Bruce residents. Meeting with constituents is one of the most important things an MP can do.

Functioning effectively on the international scene is another duty that MPs are required to perform on a regular basis. Cultural differences and political nuances can complicate this, so MPs seeking to effectively make their point must often rely on their people skills and abilities with respect to delivering a message.
(Above) Paul speaks to a parliamentarian in Uganda (1998).
(Below) Paul meets with the South African Minister of Public Administration (2002).

(Above) Charlie Penson (an Alberta MP), Charlie Hubbard (a New Brunswick MP) and Paul Steckle participate in the 2003 World Trade Organization talks in Cancun, Mexico. Agriculture, particularly the preservation of Canada's supply management system, was a key matter during the talks.
(Below) Paul Steckle and Rose-Marie Ur (MP for Lambton-Kent-Middlesex, Ontario) prepare to meet with Texas Republican Larry Combest, the Chairman of the 106th Congressional House Agriculture Committee (1999).

(Above) On October 12, 2002, Paul Steckle presents the Queen's Golden Jubilee citations to deserving local heroes on behalf of the Governor General of Canada. Recipients were Jean Marie Bennett (Bayfield), James Butchart (Paisley), Robert B. Campbell (Clinton), Robert Courtney (Ripley), Ryan Crawford (Clinton), Ada Dinney (Exeter), Douglas and Karen Dolmage (Londesboro), Eric Eastwood (Port Elgin), Carol Erb-Gingerich (Zurich), Dalton Finkbeiner (Exeter), Clayton Groves (Clinton), Brad Kirkconnell (Kincardine), William J. Kirkey (Goderich), Richard Livesey (Goderich), Meryl MacKay (Paisley), Neil McGavin (Walton), Donald McKenzie (Goderich), Helen Rintoul (Lucknow), and Herman Young (Kincardine). Paul also was decorated by the Governor General with the medal.

(Above) Paul Steckle receives a gift and the best wishes of a number of his colleagues in Ottawa, during a surprise gathering for his 64th birthday (May 10, 2006).

(Above) Left to right: Hon. Bill Graham (Interim Leader of the Liberal Party), Paul Steckle, Bob Swartman, Kevin Wilbee, Anita Swartman, and Sandy Hamamoto pose for a photo during a Liberal Party Convention in Toronto (2006).

(Above) Paul Steckle (far right) wades into a crowd of protesting farmers during an agriculture rally on Parliament Hill (2006). Agricultural issues often took centre stage during Paul's career.

(Above) Paul and former Prime Minister Pierre Elliott Trudeau share a handshake
and a word on the floor of the House of Commons (1996).

(Above) Paul Steckle and former Prime Minister Joe Clark in front of the
Commons (2000).

(Above) Left to right: Paul Szabo (MP for Mississauga South, Ontario); Eleni Bakopanos (MP for Ahuntsic, Quebec); Prime Minister Paul Martin; Paul Steckle; and Scott Brison (MP for Kings-Hants, Nova Scotia) in the Government Lobby. Prime Minister Martin surprised the MPs with a birthday cake, as these four MPs share a common birthday (2005).
(Below) House of Commons Speaker Peter Milliken and Paul visit in the Speaker's Salon.

(Above) Left to right: Steven Truscott, Paul Steckle, and Maitland Edgar talk about Truscott's murder conviction while overlooking the crime scene outside of Clinton. Paul has worked diligently over the years to help exonerate Truscott.

(Above) Left to right: Paul Steckle, Ken Scott, Bob Mann, Paul Martin, Elgin Fisher, Bob McClinchey, Wayne McClinchey, Bill McDougall. With the exception of the two Pauls, the men are members of "Wednesday Night Class," a local band that performs during Huron-Bruce (Federal) Liberal Association events.

(Above) Lifelong Liberal supporters Joe and Kathleen Semple pose with Paul Martin, Kathy Steckle, and Paul Steckle in Formosa, Ontario (September 20, 2002).
(Below) Carol Mitchell (MPP for Huron-Bruce), David Inglis (Wingham-area resident), and Paul pose for a photo during a local Liberal event.

(Above) Paul and Corn Cob Bob share a light moment in support of renewable fuels.
(Below) Paul Steckle, Goderich resident Susan MacAdam, and the crew of the newly commissioned Canadian Coast Guard Cutter Thunder Cape pose for a photo following the official christening ceremony (2005).

(Above) The infamous Steckle Christmas card photo of 2004.
(Below) In the ornate Reading Room, flanked by family and many supporters, Paul is sworn in as the MP for Huron-Bruce for a fifth and final time (February 2006).

(Above) Paul Steckle addresses a large crowd from the front steps of Parliament,
while a number of his elected colleagues listen and look on.
(Below) Paul meets with a group of future leaders on the front steps of Parliament.

(Above) Paul and a number of dedicated local volunteers, municipal officials and children officially open the new playground equipment at the Londesboro baseball diamond.
(Below) Paul Steckle meets with federal Agriculture Minister Lyle Vanclief and former Ontario Agriculture Minister (and personal friend) Jack Riddell during the International Plowing Match in Dashwood, Ontario (1999).

(Above) The private Paul Steckle.

(Above) Dr. Cal Bombay (Crossroads Christian Ministries), the Baroness Caroline Cox (Deputy Speaker of the British House of Lords), and House of Commons Speaker Gilbert Parent pose with Paul in the Centre Block of Parliament prior to the commencement of the Canadian National Prayer Breakfast (1998).

(Above) Paul Steckle participates in a "Take Note" debate on agriculture (2006). (Below) Paul indulges his other passion—fishing.

(Above) Agriculture Minister Andy Mitchell is scrummed at the Mildmay-area farm of Ralph and Jayne Dietrich (April 16, 2005), while Carol Mitchell and Paul look on.
(Below) Paul and His Holiness, the Fourteenth Dalai Lama of Tibet, enjoy coffee and conversation

Photo Credits

Cover Photo	House of Commons photographer	2007
Photo #1 (Page #148)	Taken from Paul Steckle's personal collection	1960
Photo #2 (Page #148)	Taken from Paul Steckle's personal collection	1965
Photo #3 (Page #149)	Taken from Paul Steckle's personal collection	1967
Photo #4 (Page #149)	Taken from Paul Steckle's personal collection	1971
Photo #5 (Page #150)	Taken from Paul Steckle's personal collection	1973
Photo #6 (Page #150)	Taken from Paul Steckle's personal collection	ca. 1977
Photo #7 (Page #151)	House of Commons photographer	1993
Photo #8 (Page #151)	Jean-Marc Carisse photo	1995
Photo #9 (Page #152)	House of Commons photographer	1994
Photo #10 (Page #152)	Greg McClinchey photo	1997
Photo #11 (Page #153)	Ruth Uyl photo	2001

Photo #12 (Page #153)	House of Commons photographer	2004
Photo #13 (Page #154)	House of Commons photographer	1999
Photo #14 (Page #154)	Jean-Marc Carisse photo	1997
Photo #15 (Page #155)	Greg McClinchey Photo	2005
Photo #16 (Page #155)	Greg McClinchey photo	2000
Photo #17 (Page #156)	Photo supplied by Rev. Jerry Sherman	1998
Photo #18 (Page #156)	House of Commons photographer	2002
Photo #19 (Page #157)	Taken from Paul Steckle's personal collection	2003
Photo #20 (Page #157)	Taken from Paul Steckle's personal collection	1999
Photo #21 (Page #158)	Greg McClinchey photo	2002
Photo #22 (Page #158)	Greg McClinchey photo	2006
Photo #23 (Page #159)	Greg McClinchey photo	2006
Photo #24 (Page #159)	Greg McClinchey photo	2006
Photo #25 (Page #160)	House of Commons photographer	1996
Photo #26 (Page #160)	Greg McClinchey photo	2000
Photo #27 (Page #161)	Prime Minister's photographer	2005

Photo #28 (Page #161)	House of Commons photographer	2001
Photo #29 (Page #162)	David Emslie (*Clinton News Record*) photo	2004
Photo #30 (Page #162)	Greg McClinchey photo	2002
Photo #31 (Page #163)	Huron-Bruce (Federal) Liberal Association photo	2002
Photo #32 (Page #163)	Greg McClinchey photo	2004
Photo #33 (Page #164)	Taken from Paul Steckle's personal collection	2005
Photo #34 (Page #164)	Provided by the Dep. of Fisheries and Oceans	2005
Photo #35 (Page #165)	Phil Erb photo	2004
Photo #36 (Page #165)	House of Commons photographer	2006
Photo #37 (Page #166)	Taken from Paul Steckle's personal collection	2003
Photo #38 (Page #166)	House of Commons photographer	1998
Photo #39 (Page #167)	Taken from Paul Steckle's personal collection	2005
Photo #40 (Page #167)	Taken from Paul Steckle's personal collection	1999
Photo #41 (Page #168)	Taken from Paul Steckle's personal collection	1995
Photo #42 (Page #168)	Taken from Paul Steckle's personal collection	1998
Photo #43 (Page #169)	House of Commons photographer	2006

Epilogue

Rose-Marie Ur, RNA, Member of Parliament (Retired)
Lambton-Middlesex/Lambton-Kent-Middlesex/
Middlesex-Kent-Lambton
(October 25, 1993–January 22, 2006)

I did not know Paul Steckle prior to the 1993 election. However, as time moved on and we settled into the role of elected members of parliament (Paul as the MP for Huron-Bruce, and I as the MP representing the riding to the immediate south of him), we began to get to know each other better. As our two ridings butted each other, we soon learned that we had many similar issues to deal with. This was a tremendous advantage, as it is always better to have a strong team approach when lobbying on any particular issue.

Huron-Bruce is one of the largest agricultural ridings in Ontario, so it was important to have Paul on the Agriculture Committee. He was elected—unanimously—as chair by MPs representing all parties in the House of Commons. Yes, Paul was the Liberal chair, but you would be hard pressed to find any criticism of him from the Opposition committee members. Paul was always well prepared, concise, and fair, thus earning him the respect of each committee member, regardless of his or her partisan affiliation.

Huron-Bruce is considered a rural riding. Because of this, Paul was also on the Rural Caucus Executive and attended nearly every weekly meeting. At these meetings, Paul had the opportunity to express his very sincere concerns on various issues he championed, such as financial support for farmers, strong support for supply management, funding for invasive-species control, opposing the closure of rural post offices, opposing same-sex marriage, and opposing the long-gun registry, to name only a few. He was very vocal and presented his concerns at many caucus meetings.

It was a real pleasure to work with Paul for almost 13 years; we shared many of the same concerns and values. Our families came to know each other over the years, and we all formed lasting friendships.

Finally, in my opinion, the constituents of Huron-Bruce are well served by a very professional, honest and dedicated man, a man who always put his constituents first, and not his own possible personal gain. Paul is a man of integrity and has a quality character which constituents look for when electing a person to represent them. This has resulted in and been proven by his five consecutive elections to the House of Commons.

Index

978-0-595-68351-2
0-595-68351-7

Printed in the United States
98032LV00006B/1-48/A